NYSTCE

Mathematics (004)
Test Part 2 of 2

SECRETS

Study Guide
Your Key to Exam Success

D0073696

NYSTCE Exam Review for the
New York State Teacher
Certification Examinations

TABLE OF CONTENTS

Practice Test

Practice Questions

1. Determine the number of diagonals of a dodecagon.
   a. 12
   b. 24
   c. 54
   d. 108

2. A circular bracelet contains 5 charms, A, B, C, D, and E, attached at specific points around the bracelet, with the clasp located between charms A and B. The bracelet is unclasped and stretched out into a straight line. On the resulting linear bracelet, charm C is between charms A and B, charm D is between charms A and C, and charm E is between charms C and D. Which of these statements is (are) necessarily true?

   I. The distance between charms B and E is greater than the distance between charms A and D.
   II. Charm E is between charms B and D.
   III. The distance between charms D and E is less than the distance of bracelet between charms A and C.

   a. I, II, and III
   b. II and III
   c. II only
   d. None of these is necessarily true.

3. In a town of 35,638 people, about a quarter of the population is under the age of 35. Of those, just over a third attend local K-12 schools. If the number of students in each grade is about the same, how many fourth graders likely reside in the town?
   a. Fewer than 100
   b. Between 200 and 300
   c. Between 300 and 400
   d. More than 400

4. Identical rugs are offered for sale at two local shops and one online retailer, designated Stores A, B, and C, respectively. The rug's regular sales price is $296 at Store A, $220 at Store B, and $198.00 at Store C. Stores A and B collect 8% in sales tax on any after-discount price, while Store C collects no tax but charges a $35 shipping fee. A buyer has a 30% off coupon for Store A and a $10 off coupon for Store B. Which of these lists the stores in order of lowest to highest final sales price after all discounts, taxes, and fees are applied?
   a. Store A, Store B, Store C
   b. Store B, Store C, Store A
   c. Store C, Store A, Store C
   d. Store C, Store B, Store A

5. Two companies offer monthly cell phone plans, both of which include free text messaging. Company A charges a $25 monthly fee plus five cents per minute of phone conversation, while Company B charges a $50 monthly fee and offers unlimited calling. Both companies charge the same amount when the total duration of monthly calls is
   a. 500 hours.
   b. 8 hours and 33 minutes.
   c. 8 hours and 20 minutes.
   d. 5 hours.

6. A dress is marked down by 20% and placed on a clearance rack, on which is posted a sign reading, "Take an extra 25% off already reduced merchandise." What fraction of the original price is the final sales price of the dress?
   a. $\frac{9}{20}$
   b. $\frac{11}{20}$
   c. $\frac{2}{5}$
   d. $\frac{3}{5}$

7. On a floor plan drawn at a scale of 1:100, the area of a rectangular room is 30 cm². What is the actual area of the room?
   a. 30,000 cm²
   b. 3,000 cm²
   c. 3,000 m²
   d. 30 m²

8. The ratio of employee wages and benefits to all other operational costs of a business is 2:3. If a business's operating expenses are $130,000 per month, how much money does the company spend on employee wages and benefits?
   a. $43,333.33
   b. $86,666.67
   c. $52,000.00
   d. $78,000.00

9. The path of ball thrown into the air is modeled by the first quadrant graph of the equation $h = -16t^2 + 64t + 5$, where h is the height of the ball in feet and t is time in seconds after the ball is thrown. What is the average rate of change in the ball's height with respect to time over the interval [1, 3]?
   a. 0 feet/second
   b. 48 feet/second
   c. 53 feet/second
   d. 96 feet/second

10. Zeke drove from his house to a furniture store in Atlanta and then back home along the same route. It took Zeke three hours to drive to the store. By driving an average of 20 mph faster on his return trip, Zeke was able to save an hour of diving time. What was Zeke's average driving speed on his round trip?
   a. 24 mph
   b. 48 mph
   c. 50 mph
   d. 60 mph

11. The graph below shows Aaron's distance from home at times throughout his morning run. Which of the following statements is (are) true?

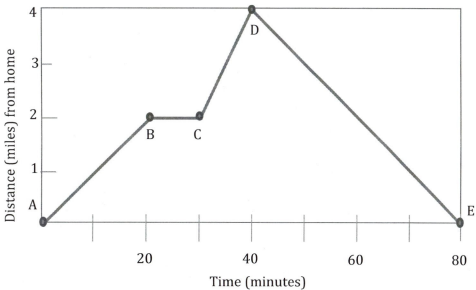

I.   Aaron's average running speed was 6 mph.
II. Aaron's running speed from point A to point B was the same as his running speed from point D to E.
III. Aaron ran a total distance of four miles.

a. I only
b. II only
c. I and II
d. I, II, and III

12. Use the operation table to determine $(a * b) * (c * d)$.

*	a	b	c	d
a	d	a	b	c
b	a	b	c	d
c	b	c	d	a
d	c	d	a	b

a. a
b. b
c. c
d. d

13. Complete the analogy.

$$x^3 \text{ is to } \sqrt[3]{y} \text{ as } ...$$

a. $x + a$ is to $x - y$.
b. e^x is to $\ln y, y > 0$.
c. $\frac{1}{x}$ is to $y, x, y \neq 0$.
d. $\sin x$ is to $\cos y$.

- 3 -

14. Which of these statements is (are) true for deductive reasoning?
   I. A general conclusion is drawn from specific instances.
   II. If the premises are true and proper reasoning is applied, the conclusion must be true.
   a. Statement I is true
   b. Statement II is true
   c. Both statements are true
   d. Neither statement is true

15. Given that premises "all a are b," "all b are d," and "no b are c" are true and that premise "all b are e" is false, determine the validity and soundness of the following arguments:
   Argument I: All a are b. No b are c. Therefore, no a are c.
   Argument II: All a are b. All d are b. Therefore, all d are a.
   Argument III: All a are b. All b are e. Therefore, all a are e.

a.

	Invalid	Valid	Sound
Argument I		X	X
Argument II	X		
Argument III		X	

b.

	Invalid	Valid	Sound
Argument I	X		
Argument II		X	X
Argument III	X		

c.

	Invalid	Valid	Sound
Argument I		X	X
Argument II		X	X
Argument III	X		

d.

	Invalid	Valid	Sound
Argument I		X	X
Argument II	X		
Argument III	X		

16. If $p \rightarrow q$ is true, which of these is also necessarily true?
   a. $q \rightarrow p$
   b. $\sim p \rightarrow \sim q$
   c. $\sim q \rightarrow \sim p$
   d. None of these

17. Given statements p and q, which of the following is the truth table for the statement $q \leftrightarrow \sim(p \wedge q)$?

a.

p	q	$q \leftrightarrow \sim(p \wedge q)$
T	T	F
T	F	T
F	T	T
F	F	T

b.

p	q	$q \leftrightarrow \sim(p \wedge q)$
T	T	T
T	F	T
F	T	T
F	F	F

c.

p	q	$q \leftrightarrow \sim(p \wedge q)$
T	T	F
T	F	F
F	T	F
F	F	T

d.

p	q	$q \leftrightarrow \sim(p \wedge q)$
T	T	F
T	F	F
F	T	T
F	F	F

18. Which of the following is the truth table for logic circuit shown below?

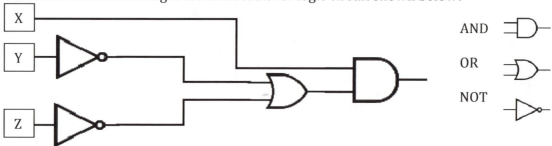

a.

X	Y	Z	Output
0	0	0	1
0	0	1	0
0	1	0	0
0	1	1	0
1	0	0	0
1	0	1	0
1	1	0	0
1	1	1	1

c.

X	Y	Z	Output
0	0	0	0
0	0	1	0
0	1	0	0
0	1	1	1
1	0	0	1
1	0	1	1
1	1	0	1
1	1	1	0

b.

X	Y	Z	Output
0	0	0	0
0	0	1	1
0	1	0	1
0	1	1	1
1	0	0	1
1	0	1	1
1	1	0	1
1	1	1	1

d.

X	Y	Z	Output
0	0	0	0
0	0	1	0
0	1	0	0
0	1	1	0
1	0	0	1
1	0	1	1
1	1	0	1
1	1	1	0

19. Which of these is a major contribution of the Babylonian civilization to the historical development of mathematics?
    a. The division of an hour into 60 minutes, and a minute into 60 seconds, and a circle into 360 degrees
    b. The development of algebra as a discipline separate from geometry
    c. The use of deductive reasoning in geometric proofs
    d. The introduction of Boolean logic and algebra

20. Which mathematician is responsible for what is often called the most remarkable and beautiful mathematical formula, $e^{i\pi} + 1 = 0$?
    a. Pythagoras
    b. Euclid
    c. Euler
    d. Fermat

21. Which of these demonstrates the relationship between the sets of prime numbers, real numbers, natural numbers, complex numbers, rational numbers, and integers?
P – Prime; ℝ – Real; ℕ – Natural; ℂ – Complex; ℚ – Rational; ℤ – Integer
   a. $\mathbb{P} \subseteq \mathbb{Q} \subseteq \mathbb{R} \subseteq \mathbb{Z} \subseteq \mathbb{C} \subseteq \mathbb{N}$
   b. $\mathbb{P} \subseteq \mathbb{N} \subseteq \mathbb{Z} \subseteq \mathbb{Q} \subseteq \mathbb{R} \subseteq \mathbb{C}$
   c. $\mathbb{C} \subseteq \mathbb{R} \subseteq \mathbb{Q} \subseteq \mathbb{Z} \subseteq \mathbb{N} \subseteq \mathbb{P}$
   d. None of these

22. To which of the following sets of numbers does −4 **NOT** belong?
   a. The set of whole numbers
   b. The set of rational numbers
   c. The set of integers
   d. The set of real numbers

23. Which of these forms a group?
   a. The set of prime numbers under addition
   b. The set of negative integers under multiplication
   c. The set of negative integers under addition
   d. The set of non-zero rational numbers under multiplication

24. Simplify $\frac{2+3i}{4-2i}$.
   a. $\frac{1}{10} + \frac{4}{5}i$
   b. $\frac{1}{10}$
   c. $\frac{7}{6} + \frac{2}{3}i$
   d. $\frac{1}{10} + \frac{3}{10}i$

25. Simplify $|(2 - 3i)^2 - (1 - 4i)|$.
   a. $\sqrt{61}$
   b. $-6 - 8i$
   c. $6 + 8i$
   d. 10

26. Which of these sets forms a group under multiplication?
   a. $\{-i, 0, i\}$
   b. $\{-1, 1, i, -i\}$
   c. $\{i, 1\}$
   d. $\{i, -i, 1\}$

27. The set $\{a, b, c, d\}$ forms a group under operation #. Which of these statements is (are) true about the group?

#	a	b	c	d
a	c	d	b	a
b	d	c	a	b
c	b	a	d	c
d	a	b	c	d

I.   The identity element of the group is d.
II.   The inverse of c is c.
III. The operation # is commutative.

a. I
b. III
c. I, III
d. I, II, III

28. If the square of twice the sum of x and three is equal to the product of twenty-four and x, which of these is a possible value of x?

a. $6 + 3\sqrt{2}$
b. $\frac{3}{2}$
c. $-3i$
d. -3

29. Given that x is a prime number and that the greatest common factor of x and y is greater than 1, compare the two quantities.

Quantity A   Quantity B

y the least common multiple of x and y

a. Quantity A is greater.
b. Quantity B is greater.
c. The two quantities are the same.
d. The relationship cannot be determined from the given information.

30. If a, b, and c are even integers and $3a^2 + 9b^3 = c$, which of these is the largest number which must be factor of c?

a. 2
b. 3
c. 6
d. 12

- 8 -

31. Which of these relationships represents y as a function of x?

    a. $x = y^2$

    b.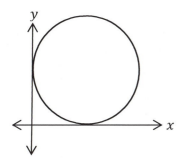

    c. $y = [\![x]\!]s$

    d.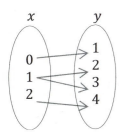

32. Express the area of the given triangle as a function of x.

    a. $A(x) = 3x$

    b. $A(x) = \dfrac{x\sqrt{36-x^2}}{2}$

    c. $A(x) = \dfrac{x^2}{2}$

    d. $A(x) = 18 - \dfrac{x^2}{2}$

33. Find $[g \circ f]x$ when $f(x) = 2x + 4$ and $g(x) = x^2 - 3x + 2$.

    a. $4x^2 + 10x + 6$

    b. $2x^2 - 6x + 8$

    c. $4x^2 + 13x + 18$

    d. $2x^2 - 3x + 6$

- 9 -

34. Given the partial table of values for $f(x)$ and $g(x)$, find $f(g(-4))$. (Assume that $f(x)$ and $g(x)$ are the simplest polynomials that fit the data.)

x	f(x)	g(x)
-2	8	1
-1	2	3
0	0	5
1	2	7
2	8	9

a. 69
b. 31
c. 18
d. –3

35. If $f(x)$ and $g(x)$ are inverse functions, which of these is the value of x when $f(g(x)) = 4$?
a. –4
b. $\frac{1}{4}$
c. 2
d. 4

36. Determine which pair of equations are **NOT** inverses.
a. $y = x + 6$; $y = x - 6$
b. $y = 2x + 3$; $y = 2x - 3$
c. $y = \frac{2x+3}{x-1}$; $y = \frac{x+3}{x-2}$
d. $y = \frac{x-1}{2}$; $y = 2x + 1$

37. Which of these statements is (are) true for function $g(x)$?

$$g(x) \begin{cases} 2x - 1 & x \geq 2 \\ -x + 3 & x < 2 \end{cases}$$

I. $g(3) = 0$
II. The graph of $g(x)$ is discontinuous at $x = 2$.
III. The range of $g(x)$ is all real numbers.

a. II
b. III
c. I, II
d. II, III

38. Which of the following piecewise functions can describe the graph below?

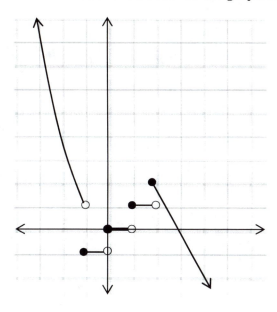

a. $f(x) \begin{cases} x^2 & x < -1 \\ [\![x]\!] & -1 \le x < 2 \\ -2x + 6 & x \ge 2 \end{cases}$

b. $f(x) \begin{cases} x^2 & x \le -1 \\ [\![x]\!] & -1 \le x \le 2 \\ -2x + 6 & x > 2 \end{cases}$

c. $f(x) \begin{cases} (x + 1)^2 & x < -1 \\ [\![x]\!] + 1 & -1 \le x < 2 \\ -2x + 6 & x \ge 2 \end{cases}$

d. $f(x) \begin{cases} (x + 1)^2 & x < -1 \\ [\![x - 1]\!] & -1 \le x < 2 \\ -2x + 6 & x \ge 2 \end{cases}$

39. Which of the following could be the graph of $y = a(x + b)(x + c)^2$ if $a > 0$?

a.

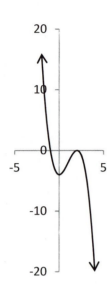

c.

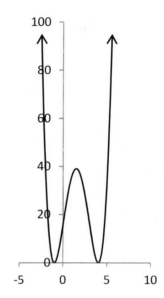

b.

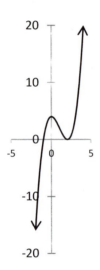

d.

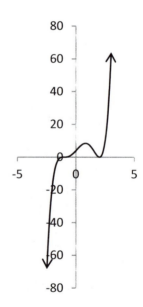

40. A school is selling tickets to its production of *Annie Get Your Gun*. Student tickets cost $3 each, and non-student tickets are $5 each. In order to offset the costs of the production, the school must earn at least $300 in ticket sales. Which graph shows the number of tickets the school must sell to offset production costs?

a.

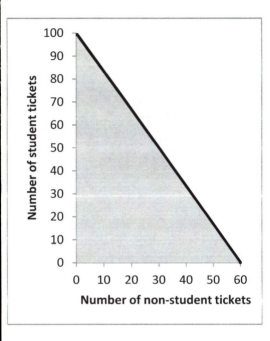

c.

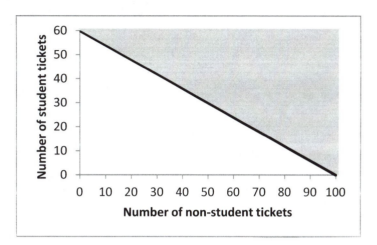

b.

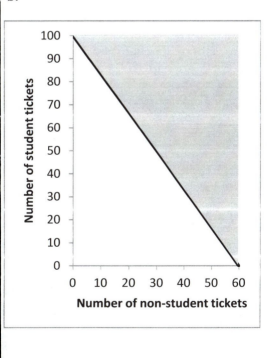

d.

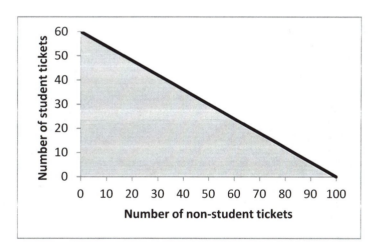

41. Which of these is the equation graphed below?

    a. $y = -2x^2 - 4x + 1$
    b. $y = -x^2 - 2x + 5$
    c. $y = -x^2 - 2x + 2$
    d. $y = -\frac{1}{2}x^2 - x + \frac{5}{2}$

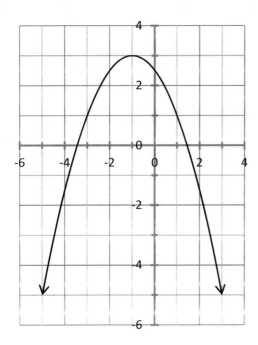

42. Solve $7x^2 + 6x = -2$.

    a. $x = \frac{-3 \pm \sqrt{23}}{7}$
    b. $x = \pm i\sqrt{5}$
    c. $x = \pm \frac{2i\sqrt{2}}{7}$
    d. $x = \frac{-3 \pm i\sqrt{5}}{7}$

43. Solve the system of equations.

$$3x + 4y = 2$$
$$2x + 6y = -2$$

    a. $\left(0, \frac{1}{2}\right)$
    b. $\left(\frac{2}{5}, \frac{1}{5}\right)$
    c. $(2, -1)$
    d. $\left(-1, \frac{5}{4}\right)$

44. Which system of linear inequalities has no solution?
   a. $x - y < 3$
      $x - y \geq -3$
   b. $y \leq 6 - 2x$
      $\frac{1}{3}y + \frac{2}{3}x \geq 2$
   c. $6x + 2y \leq 12$
      $3x \geq 8 - y$
   d. $x + 4y \leq -8$
      $y + 4x > -8$

45. The cost of admission to a theme park is shown below.

Under age 10	Ages 10-55	Over age 65
$15	$25	$20

Yesterday, the theme park sold 810 tickets and earned $14,500. There were twice as many children under 10 at the park as there were other visitors. If x, y, and z represent the number of $15, $25, and $20 tickets sold, respectively, which of the following matrix equations can be used to find the number of each type of ticket sold?

a. $\begin{bmatrix} 1 & 1 & 1 \\ 15 & 25 & 20 \\ 1 & -2 & -2 \end{bmatrix} \begin{bmatrix} x \\ y \\ z \end{bmatrix} = \begin{bmatrix} 810 \\ 14500 \\ 0 \end{bmatrix}$

b. $\begin{bmatrix} 1 & 1 & 1 \\ 15 & 25 & 20 \\ 1 & -2 & -2 \end{bmatrix} \begin{bmatrix} 810 \\ 14500 \\ 0 \end{bmatrix} = \begin{bmatrix} x \\ y \\ z \end{bmatrix}$

c. $\begin{bmatrix} 1 & 15 & 1 \\ 1 & 25 & -2 \\ 1 & 20 & -2 \end{bmatrix} \begin{bmatrix} x \\ y \\ z \end{bmatrix} = \begin{bmatrix} 810 \\ 14500 \\ 0 \end{bmatrix}$

d. $\begin{bmatrix} 1 & 15 & 1 \\ 1 & 25 & -2 \\ 1 & 20 & -2 \end{bmatrix} \begin{bmatrix} 810 \\ 14500 \\ 0 \end{bmatrix} = \begin{bmatrix} x \\ y \\ z \end{bmatrix}$

46. Solve the system of equations.
$$2x - 4y + z = 10$$
$$-3x + 2y - 4z = -7$$
$$x + y - 3z = -1$$

   a. $(-1, -3, 0)$
   b. $(1, -2, 0)$
   c. $(-\frac{3}{4}, -\frac{21}{8}, -1)$
   d. No solution

47. Solve $x^4 + 64 = 20x^2$.
   a. $x = \{2, 4\}$
   b. $x = \{-2, 2, -4, 4\}$
   c. $x = \{2i, 4i\}$
   d. $x = \{-2i, 2i, -4i, 4i\}$

48. Solve $3x^3y^2 - 45x^2y = 15x^3y - 9x^2y^2$ for x and y.
    a. $x = \{0, -3\}$, $y = \{0, 5\}$
    b. $x = \{0\}$, $y = \{0\}$
    c. $x = \{0, -3\}$, $y = \{0\}$
    d. $x = \{0\}$, $y = \{0, 5\}$

49. Which of these statements is true for functions $f(x), g(x)$, and $h(x)$?
$$f(x) = 2x - 2$$
$$g(x) = 2x^2 - 2$$
$$h(x) = 2x^3 - 2$$
    a. The degree of each polynomial function is 2.
    b. The leading coefficient of each function is –2.
    c. Each function has exactly one real zero at x = 1.
    d. None of these is true for functions f(x), g(x), and h(x).

50. Which of these can be modeled by a quadratic function?
    a. The path of a sound wave
    b. The path of a bullet
    c. The distance an object travels over time when the rate is constant
    d. Radioactive decay

51. Which of these is equivalent to $\log_y 256$ if $2 \log_4 y + \log_4 16 = 3$?
    a. 16
    b. 8
    c. 4
    d. 2

52. Simplify $\dfrac{(x^2y)(2xy^{-2})^3}{16x^5y^2} + \dfrac{3}{xy}$

    a. $\dfrac{3x+24y^6}{8xy^7}$

    b. $\dfrac{x+6y^6}{2xy^7}$

    c. $\dfrac{x+24y^5}{8xy^6}$

    d. $\dfrac{x+6y^5}{2xy^6}$

53. Given: $f(x) = 10^x$. If $f(x) = 5$, which of these approximates x?
    a. 100,000
    b. 0.00001
    c. 0.7
    d. 1.6

54. Which of these could be the equation of the function graphed below?
   a. $f(x) = x^2$
   b. $f(x) = \sqrt{x}$
   c. $f(x) = 2^x$
   d. $f(x) = \log_2 x$

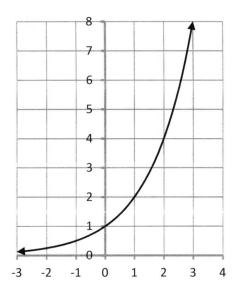

55. Which of these statements is **NOT** necessarily true when $f(x) = \log_b x$ and $b > 1$?
   a. The x-intercept of the graph of f(x) is 1.
   b. The graph of f(x) passes through $(b, 1)$
   c. $f(x) < 0$ when x < 1
   d. If $g(x) = b^x$, the graph of f(x) is symmetric to the graph of g(x) with respect to y = x.

56. A colony of *Escherichia coli* is inoculated from a Petri dish into a test tube containing 50 mL of nutrient broth. The test tube is placed in a 37°C incubator/shaker; after one hour, the number of bacteria in the test tube is determined to be 8×10^6. Given that the doubling time of *E. coli* is 20 minutes with agitation at 37°C, approximately how many bacteria should the test tube contain after eight hours of growth?
   a. 2.56×10^8
   b. 2.05×10^9
   c. 1.7×10^{10}
   d. 1.7×10^{13}

57. The strength of an aqueous acid solution is measured by pH. $pH = -\log[H^+]$, where $[H^+]$ is the molar concentration of hydronium ions in the solution. A solution is acidic if its pH is less than 7. The lower the pH, the stronger the acid; for example, gastric acid, which has a pH of about 1, is a much stronger acid than urine, which has a pH of about 6. How many times stronger is an acid with a pH of 3 than an acid with pH of 5?
   a. 2
   b. 20
   c. 100
   d. 1000

58. Simplify $\sqrt{\dfrac{-28x^6}{27y^5}}$.

    a. $\dfrac{2x^3 i\sqrt{21y}}{9y^3}$

    b. $\dfrac{2x^3 i\sqrt{21y}}{27y^4}$

    c. $\dfrac{-2x^3\sqrt{21y}}{9y^3}$

    d. $\dfrac{12x^3 yi\sqrt{7}}{27y^2}$

59. Which of these does **NOT** have a solution set of $\{x: -1 \le x \le 1\}$?

    a. $-4 \le 2 + 3(x - 1) \le 2$

    b. $-2x^2 + 2 \ge x^2 - 1$

    c. $\dfrac{11 - |3x|}{7} \ge 2$

    d. $3|2x| + 4 \le 10$

60. Solve $2 - \sqrt{x} = \sqrt{x - 20}$.

    a. $x = 6$

    b. $x = 36$

    c. $x = 144$

    d. No solution

61. Solve $\dfrac{x-2}{x-1} = \dfrac{x-1}{x+1} + \dfrac{2}{x-1}$.

    a. $x = 2$

    b. $x = -5$

    c. $x = 1$

    d. No solution

62. Which of these equations is represented by the graph below?

a. $y = \dfrac{3}{x^2 - x - 2}$

b. $y = \dfrac{3x+3}{x^2 - x - 2}$

c. $y = \dfrac{1}{x+1} + \dfrac{1}{x-2}$

d. None of these

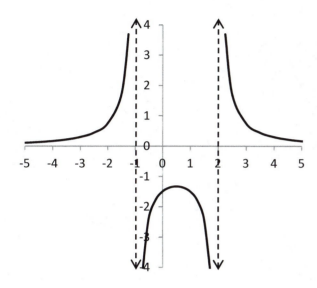

63. Which of the graphs shown represents $f(x) = -2|-x+4| - 1$?

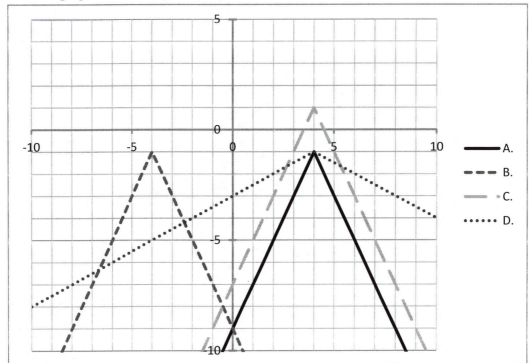

64. Which of these functions includes 1 as an element of the domain and 2 as an element of the range?

a. $y = \dfrac{1}{x-1} + 1$

b. $y = -\sqrt{x+2} - 1$

c. $y = |x+2| - 3$

d. $y = \begin{cases} x, & x < 1 \\ -x - 3, & x \geq 1 \end{cases}$

65. Which of the following statements is (are) true when $f(x) = \dfrac{x^2-x-6}{x^3+2x^2-x-2}$?

   I. The graph f(x) has vertical asymptotes at $x = -2$, $x = -1$, and $x = 1$.
   II. The x- and y-intercepts of the graph of $f(x)$ are both 3.

a. I

b. II

c. I and II

d. Neither statement is true.

66. In the 1600s, Galileo Galilei studied the motion of pendulums and discovered that the period of a pendulum, the time it takes to complete one full swing, is a function of the square root of the length of its string: $2\pi\sqrt{\frac{L}{g}}$, where L is the length of the string and g is the acceleration due to gravity.

Consider two pendulums released from the same pivot point and at the same angle, $\theta = 30°$. Pendulum 1 has a mass of 100 g, while Pendulum 2 has a mass of 200 g. If Pendulum 1 has a period four times the period of Pendulum 2, what is true of the lengths of the pendulums' strings?
    a. The length of Pendulum 1's string is four times the length of Pendulum 2's string.
    b. The length of Pendulum 1's string is eight times the length of Pendulum 2's string.
    c. The length of Pendulum 1's string is sixteen times the length of Pendulum 2's string.
    d. The length of Pendulum 1's string is less than the length of Pendulum 2's string.

67. At today's visit to her doctor, Josephine was prescribed a liquid medication with instructions to take 25 cc's every four hours. She filled the prescription on her way to work, but when it came time to take the medicine, she realized that the pharmacist did not include a measuring cup. Josephine estimated that the plastic spoon in her desk drawer was about the same size as a teaspoon and decided to use it to measure the approximate dosage. She recalled that one cubic centimeter (cc) is equal to one milliliter (mL) but was not sure how many milliliters were in a teaspoon. So, she noted that a two-liter bottle of soda contains about the same amount as a half-gallon container of milk and applied her knowledge of the customary system of measurement to determine how many teaspoons of medicine to take. Which of these calculations might she have used to approximate her dosage?
    a. $25 \cdot \frac{1}{1000} \cdot \frac{2}{0.5} \cdot 16 \cdot 48$
    b. $25 \cdot \frac{1}{100} \cdot \frac{0.5}{2} \cdot 16 \cdot 4 \cdot 12$
    c. $\frac{1000}{25} \cdot \frac{0.5}{2} \cdot 16 \cdot 4 \cdot 12$
    d. $\frac{25}{1000} \cdot \frac{1}{4} \cdot 16 \cdot 48$

68. If 1" on a map represents 60 ft, how many yards apart are two points if the distance between the points on the map is 10"?
    a. 1800
    b. 600
    c. 200
    d. 2

69. Roxana walks x meters west and $x + 20$ meters south to get to her friend's house. On a neighborhood map which has a scale of 1cm:10 m, the distance between Roxana's house and her friend's house is 10 cm. How far did Roxana walk to her friend's house?
  a. 60 m
  b. 80 m
  c. 100 m
  d. 140 m

70. For ΔABC, what is AB?
  a. 3
  b. 10
  c. 12
  d. 15

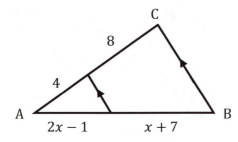

71. To test the accuracy and precision of two scales, a student repeatedly measured the mass of a 10 g standard and recorded these results.

	Trial 1	Trial 2	Trial 3	Trial 4
Scale 1	9.99 g	9.98 g	10.02g	10.01g
Scale 2	10.206 g	10.209 g	10.210 g	10.208 g

Which of these conclusions about the scales is true?
  a. Scale 1 has an average percent error of 0.15%, and Scale 2 has an average percent error of 2.08%. Scale 1 is more accurate and precise than Scale 2.
  b. Scale 1 has an average percent error of 0.15%, and Scale 2 has an average percent error of 2.08%. Scale 1 is more accurate than Scale 2; however, Scale 2 is more precise.
  c. Scale 1 has an average percent error of 0%, and Scale 2 has an average percent error of 2.08%. Scale 1 is more accurate and precise than Scale 2.
  D. Scale 1 has an average percent error of 0%, and Scale 2 has an average percent error of 2.08%. Scale 1 is more accurate than Scale 2; however, Scale 2 is more precise.

72. A developer decides to build a fence around a neighborhood park, which is positioned on a rectangular lot. Rather than fencing along the lot line, he fences x feet from each of the lot's boundaries. By fencing a rectangular space 141 yd^2 smaller than the lot, the developer saves $432 in fencing materials, which cost $12 per linear foot. How much does he spend?
  a. $160
  b. $456
  c. $3,168
  d. The answer cannot be determined from the given information.

73. Natasha designs a square pyramidal tent for her children. Each of the sides of the square base measures x ft, and the tent's height is h feet. If Natasha were to increase by 1 ft the length of each side of the base, how much more interior space would the tent have?

a. $\frac{h(x^2+2x+1)}{3}$ ft^3

b. $\frac{h(2x+1)}{3}$ ft^3

c. $\frac{x^2h+3}{3}$ ft^3

d. 1 ft^3

74. A rainbow pattern is designed from semi-circles as shown below.

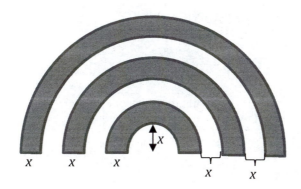

Which of the following gives the area A of the shaded region as a function of x?

a. $A = \frac{21x^2\pi}{2}$

b. $A = 21x^2\pi$

c. $A = 42x^2\pi$

d. $A = 82x^2\pi$

75. Categorize the following statements as axioms of Euclidean, hyperbolic, or elliptical geometry.

I. In a plane, for any line l and point A not on l, no lines which pass through A intersect l.

II. In a plane, for any line l and point A not on l, exactly one line which passes through A does not intersect l.

III. In a plane, for any line l and point A not on l, all lines which pass through A intersect l.

a.

Statement I	Elliptical geometry
Statement II	Euclidean geometry
Statement III	Hyperbolic geometry

b.

Statement I	Hyperbolic geometry
Statement II	Euclidean geometry
Statement III	Elliptical geometry

c.

Statement I	Hyperbolic geometry
Statement II	Elliptical geometry
Statement III	Euclidean geometry

d.

Statement I	Elliptical geometry
Statement II	Hyperbolic geometry
Statement III	Euclidean geometry

76. As shown below, four congruent isosceles trapezoids are positioned such that they form an arch. Find x for the indicated angle.

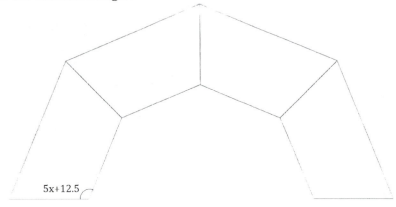

a. x = 11
b. x = 20
c. x = 24.5
d. The value of x cannot be determined from the information given.

77. A circle is inscribed inside quadrilateral $ABCD$. $\overline{CD}$ is bisected by the point at which it is tangent to the circle. If $AB = 14, BC = 10, DC = 8$, then
    a. AD = 11.
    b. AD = $2\sqrt{34}$.
    c. AD = 12.
    d. AD = 17.5.

78. Which of the following equations gives the area A of the triangle below as a function of a and b?

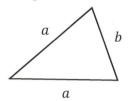

    a. $\dfrac{2a^2-b^2}{4}$

    b. $\dfrac{ab-a^2}{2}$

    c. $\dfrac{b\sqrt{a^2-b^2}}{2}$

    d. $\dfrac{b\sqrt{4a^2-b^2}}{4}$

79. Given the figure and the following information, find DE to the nearest tenth.
$\overline{AD}$ is an altitude of $\triangle ABC$
$\overline{DE}$ is an altitude of triangle $\triangle ADC$
$BD \cong DC$
$BC = 24; AD = 5$

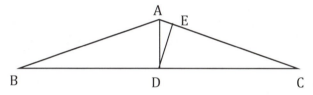

    a. 4.2
    b. 4.6
    c. 4.9
    d. 5.4

80. A cube inscribed in a sphere has a volume of 64 cubic units. What is the volume of the sphere in cubic units?
    a. $4\pi\sqrt{3}$
    b. $8\pi\sqrt{3}$
    c. $32\pi\sqrt{3}$
    d. $256\pi\sqrt{3}$

Questions 81 and 82 are based on the following proof:

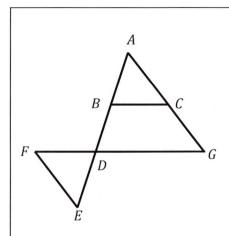

Statement	Reason
1. $\overline{BC}\|\overline{FG}$	Given
2.	
3. $\overline{FD} \cong \overline{BC}$	Given
4. $\overline{AB} \cong \overline{DE}$	Given
5. $\triangle ABC \cong \triangle EDF$	___81.___
6. ___82.___	
7. $\overline{FE}\|\overline{AG}$	

Given: $\overline{BC}\|\overline{FG}$; $\overline{FD} \cong \overline{BC}$; $\overline{AB} \cong \overline{DE}$
Prove: $\overline{FE}\|\overline{AG}$

81. Which of the following justifies step 5 in the proof above?
   a. AAS
   b. SSS
   c. ASA
   d. SAS

82. Step 6 in the above proof should contain which of the following statements?
   a. $\angle BAC \cong \angle DEF$
   b. $\angle ABC \cong \angle EDF$
   c. $\angle ACB \cong \angle EFD$
   d. $\angle GDA \cong \angle EDF$

83. Which of these is **NOT** a net of a cube?

a.
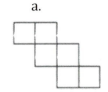

b.
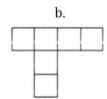

c.
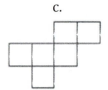

d.
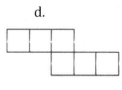

84. Identify the cross-section polygon formed by a plane containing the given points on the cube.
    a. Rectangle
    b. Trapezoid
    c. Pentagon
    d. Hexagon

85. Which of these represents the equation of a sphere which is centered in the xyz-space at the point (1, 0, -2) and which has a volume of 36π cubic units?
    a. $x^2 + y^2 + z^2 - 2x + 4z = 4$
    b. $x^2 + y^2 + z^2 + 2x - 4z = 4$
    c. $x^2 + y^2 + z^2 - 2x + 4z = -2$
    d. $x^2 + y^2 + z^2 + 2x - 4z = 2$

86. A triangle has vertices (0,0,0), (0,0,4), and (0,3,0) in the xyz-space. In cubic units, what is the difference in the volume of the solid formed by rotating the triangle about the z-axis and the solid formed by rotating the triangle about the y-axis?
    a. 0
    b. 4π
    c. 5π
    d. 25

87. If the midpoint of a line segment graphed on the xy-coordinate plane is $(3, -1)$ and the slope of the line segment is -2, which of these is a possible endpoint of the line segment?
    a. $(-1,1)$
    b. $(0, -5)$
    c. $(7,1)$
    d. $(5, -5)$

88. The vertices of a polygon are $(2,3), (8,1), (6, -5)$, and $(0, -3)$. Which of the following describes the polygon most specifically?
    a. Parallelogram
    b. Rhombus
    c. Rectangle
    d. Square

89. What is the radius of the circle defined by the equation $x^2 + y^2 - 10x + 8y + 29 = 0$?
    a. $2\sqrt{3}$
    b. $2\sqrt{5}$
    b. $\sqrt{29}$
    d. 12

90. Which of these describes the graph of the equation $2x^2 - 3y^2 - 12x + 6y - 15 = 0$?
    a. Circular
    b. Elliptical
    c. Parabolic
    d. Hyperbolic

91. The graph of $f(x)$ is a parabola with a focus of (a, b) and a directrix of $y = -b$, and $g(x)$ represents a transformation of $f(x)$. If the vertex of the graph of $g(x)$ is $(a, 0)$, which of these is a possible equation for $g(x)$ for nonzero integers a and b?

    a. $g(x) = f(x) + b$
    b. $g(x) = -f(x)$
    c. $g(x) = f(x + a)$
    d. $g(x) = f(x - a) + b$

92. A triangle with vertices $A(-4,2), B(-1,3)$, and $C(-5,7)$ is reflected across $y = x + 2$ to give $\Delta A'B'C'$, which is subsequently reflected across the y-axis to give $\Delta A''B''C''$. Which of these statements is true?

    a. A 90° rotation of ΔABC about $(-2,0)$ gives $\Delta A''B''C''$.
    b. A reflection of ΔABC about the x-axis gives $\Delta A''B''C''$.
    c. A 270° rotation of ΔABC about $(0,2)$ gives $\Delta A''B''C''$.
    d. A translation of ΔABC two units down gives $\Delta A''B''C''$.

93. For which of these does a rotation of 120° about the center of the polygon map the polygon onto itself?

    a. Square
    b. Regular hexagon
    c. Regular octagon
    d. Regular decagon

94. Line segment $\overline{PQ}$ has endpoints (a, b) and (c, b). If $\overline{P'Q'}$ is the translation of $\overline{PQ}$ along a diagonal line such that P' is located at point (c, d), what is the area of quadrilateral $PP'Q'Q$?

    a. $|a - c| \cdot |b - d|$
    b. $|a - b| \cdot |c - d|$
    c. $|a - d| \cdot |b - c|$
    d. $(a - c)^2$

95. For the right triangle below, which of the following is a true statement of equality?

    a. $\tan B = \dfrac{a}{b}$

    b. $\cos B = \dfrac{a\sqrt{a^2+b^2}}{a^2+b^2}$

    c. $\sec B = \dfrac{\sqrt{a^2+b^2}}{b}$

    d. $\csc B = \dfrac{a^2+b^2}{b}$

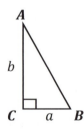

96. A man looks out of a window of a tall building at a 45° angle of depression and sees his car in the parking lot. When he turns his gaze downward to a 60° angle of depression, he sees his wife's car. If his car is parked 60 feet from his wife's car, about how far from the building did his wife park her car?

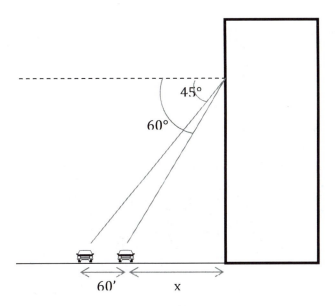

    a. 163 feet
    b. 122 feet
    c. 82 feet
    d. 60 feet

97. What is the exact value of $\tan(-\frac{2\pi}{3})$?
    a. $\sqrt{3}$
    b. $-\sqrt{3}$
    c. $\frac{\sqrt{3}}{3}$
    d. 1

98. If $\sin\theta = \frac{1}{2}$ when $\frac{\pi}{2} < \theta < \pi$, what is the value of θ?
    a. $\frac{\pi}{6}$

    b. $\frac{\pi}{3}$

    c. $\frac{2\pi}{3}$

    d. $\frac{5\pi}{6}$

99. Which of the following expressions is equal to $\cos\theta \cot\theta$?
   a. $\sin\theta$
   b. $\sec\theta \tan\theta$
   c. $\csc\theta - \sin\theta$
   d. $\sec\theta - \sin\theta$

100. Solve $\sec^2\theta = 2\tan\theta$ for $0 < \theta \le 2\pi$.
   a. $\theta = \frac{\pi}{6}$ or $\frac{7\pi}{6}$
   b. $\theta = \frac{\pi}{4}$ or $\frac{5\pi}{4}$
   c. $\theta = \frac{3\pi}{4}$ or $\frac{7\pi}{4}$
   d. There is no solution to the equation.

101. A car is driving along the highway at a constant speed when it runs over a pebble, which becomes lodged in one of the tire's treads. If this graph represent the height h of the pebble above the road in inches as a function of time t in seconds, which of these statements is true?

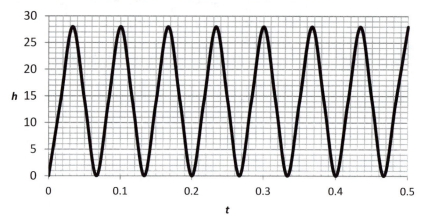

   a. The outer radius of the tire is 14 inches, and the tire rotates 900 times per minute.
   b. The outer radius of the tire is 28 inches, and the tire rotates 900 times per minute.
   c. The outer radius of the tire is 14 inches, and the tire rotates 120 times per minute.
   d. The outer radius of the tire is 28 inches, and the tire rotates 120 times per minute.

Below are graphed functions $f(x) = a_1 \sin(b_1 x)$ and $g(x) = a_2 \cos(b_2 x)$; a_1 and a_2 are integers, and b_1 and b_2 are positive rational numbers. Use this information to answer questions 102-103:

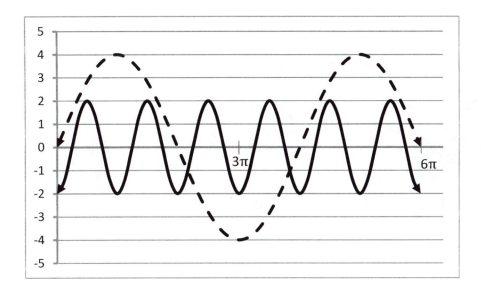

102. Which of the following statements is true?
    a. The graph of f(x) is represented by a solid line.
    b. The amplitude of the graph of g(x) is 4.
    c. $0 < b_1 < 1$.
    d. $b_2 = \pi$.

103. Which of the following statements is true?
    a. $0 < a_2 < a_1$
    b. $a_2 < 0 < a_1$
    c. $0 < a_1 < a_2$
    d. $a_2 < a_1 < 0$

104. A weight suspended on a spring is at its equilibrium point five inches above the top of a table. When the weight is pulled down two inches, it bounces above the equilibrium point and returns to the point from which it was released in one second. Which of these can be used to model the weight's height h above the table as a function of time t in seconds?
    a. $h = -2 \cos(2\pi t) + 5$
    b. $h = 5 \sin(t) - 2$
    c. $h = -2 \sin(2\pi t) + 5$
    d. $h = -2\cos(0.5\pi t) + 3$

105. Evaluate $\lim_{x \to -3} \frac{x^3 + 3x^2 - x - 3}{x^2 - 9}$.
    a. 0
    b. $\frac{1}{3}$
    c. $-\frac{4}{3}$
    d. ∞

106. Evaluate $\lim_{x \to \infty} \frac{x^2+2x-3}{2x^2+1}$.

    a. 0

    b. $\frac{1}{2}$

    c. -3

    d. ∞

107. Evaluate $\lim_{x \to 3^+} \frac{|x-3|}{3-x}$.

    a. 0

    b. –1

    c. 1

    d. ∞

108. If $f(x) = \frac{1}{4}x^2 - 3$, find the slope of the line tangent to graph of $f(x)$ at $x = 2$.

    a. –2

    b. 0

    c. 1

    d. 4

109. If $f(x) = 2x^3 - 3x^2 + 4$, what is $\lim_{h \to 0} \frac{f(2+h)-f(2)}{h}$?

    a. -4

    b. 4

    c. 8

    d. 12

110. Find the derivative of $f(x) = e^{3x^2-1}$.

    a. $6xe^{6x}$

    b. e^{3x^2-1}

    c. $(3x^2 - 1)e^{3x^2-2}$

    d. $6xe^{3x^2-1}$

111. Find the derivative of $f(x) = \ln(2x + 1)$.

    a. $\frac{1}{2x+1}$

    b. $2e^{2x+1}$

    c. $\frac{2}{2x+1}$

    d. $\frac{1}{2}$

112. For functions $f(x)$, $g(x)$, and $h(x)$, determine the limit of the function as x approaches 2 and the continuity of the function at $x = 2$.

a.

$\lim\limits_{x\to2+} f(x) = 4$ $\lim\limits_{x\to2-} f(x) = 2$ $f(2) = 2$	$\lim\limits_{x\to2} f(x)$ does not exist	The function f(x) is discontinuous at 2.
$\lim\limits_{x\to2+} g(x) = 2$ $\lim\limits_{x\to2-} g(x) = 2$ $g(2) = 4$	$\lim\limits_{x\to2} g(x) = 2$	The function g(x) is discontinuous at 2.
$\lim\limits_{x\to2+} h(x) = 2$ $\lim\limits_{x\to2-} h(x) = 2$ $h(2) = 2$	$\lim\limits_{x\to2} h(x) = 2$	The function h(x) is continuous at 2.

b.

$\lim\limits_{x\to2+} f(x) = 4$ $\lim\limits_{x\to2-} f(x) = 2$ $f(2) = 2$	$\lim\limits_{x\to2} f(x)$ does not exist	The function f(x) is continuous at 2.
$\lim\limits_{x\to2+} g(x) = 2$ $\lim\limits_{x\to2-} g(x) = 2$ $g(2) = 4$	$\lim\limits_{x\to2} g(x)$ does not exist	The function g(x) is continuous at 2.
$\lim\limits_{x\to2+} h(x) = 2$ $\lim\limits_{x\to2-} h(x) = 2$ $h(2) = 2$	$\lim\limits_{x\to2} h(x) = 2$	The function h(x) is continuous at 2.

c.

$\lim\limits_{x \to 2+} f(x) = 4$ $\lim\limits_{x \to 2-} f(x) = 2$ $f(2) = 2$	$\lim\limits_{x \to 2} f(x) = 2$	The function f(x) is continuous at 2.
$\lim\limits_{x \to 2+} g(x) = 2$ $\lim\limits_{x \to 2-} g(x) = 2$ $g(2) = 4$	$\lim\limits_{x \to 2} g(x) = 2$	The function g(x) is discontinuous at 2.
$\lim\limits_{x \to 2+} h(x) = 2$ $\lim\limits_{x \to 2-} h(x) = 2$ $h(2) = 2$	$\lim\limits_{x \to 2} h(x) = 2$	The function h(x) is continuous at 2.

d.

$\lim\limits_{x \to 2+} f(x) = 4$ $\lim\limits_{x \to 2-} f(x) = 2$ $f(2) = 2$	$\lim\limits_{x \to 2} f(x) = 2$	The function f(x) is discontinuous at 2.
$\lim\limits_{x \to 2+} g(x) = 2$ $\lim\limits_{x \to 2-} g(x) = 2$ $g(2) = 4$	$\lim\limits_{x \to 2} g(x) = 2$	The function g(x) is discontinuous at 2.
$\lim\limits_{x \to 2+} h(x) = 2$ $\lim\limits_{x \to 2-} h(x) = 2$ $h(2) = 2$	$\lim\limits_{x \to 2} h(x) = 2$	The function h(x) is continuous at 2.

113. Find $f''(x)$ if $f(x) = 2x^4 - 4x^3 + 2x^2 - x + 1$.
    a. $24x^2 - 24x + 4$
    b. $8x^3 - 12x^2 + 4x - 1$
    c. $32x^2 - 36x^2 + 8$
    d. $\frac{2}{5}x^5 - x^4 + \frac{2}{3}x^3 - \frac{1}{2}x^2 + x + c$

114. If $f(x) = 4x^3 - x^2 - 4x + 2$, which of the following statements is(are) true of its graph?
    I. The point $\left(-\frac{1}{2}, 3\frac{1}{4}\right)$ is a relative maximum.

    II. The graph of f is concave upward on the interval $\left(-\infty, \frac{1}{2}\right)$.
    a. I
    b. II
    c. I and II
    d. Neither I nor II

115. Suppose the path of a baseball hit straight up from three feet above the ground is modeled by the first quadrant graph of the function $h = -16t^2 + 50t + 3$, where t is the flight time of the ball in seconds and h is the height of the ball in feet. What is the velocity of the ball two seconds after it is hit?
    a. 39 ft/s upward
    b. 19.5 ft/s upward
    c. 19.5 ft/s downward
    d. 14 ft/s downward

116. A manufacturer wishes to produce a cylindrical can which can hold up to 0.5 L of liquid. To the nearest tenth, what is the radius of the can which requires the least amount of material to make?
    a. 2.8 cm
    b. 4.3 cm
    c. 5.0 cm
    d. 9.2 cm

117. Approximate the area A under the curve by using a Riemann sum with $\Delta x = 1$.

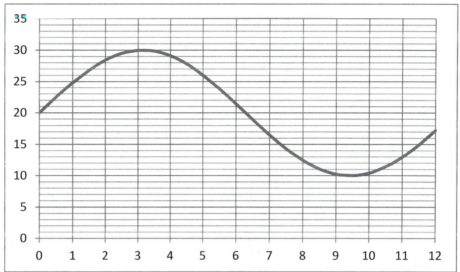

a. $209 < A < 211$
b. $230 < A < 235$
c. $238 < A < 241$
d. $246 < A < 250$

118. To the nearest hundredth, what is the area in square units under the curve of $f(x) = \frac{1}{x}$ on $[1,2]$?
a. 0.50
b. 0.69
c. 1.30
d. 1.50

119. Calculate $\int 3x^2 + 2x - 1 \ dx$.
a. $x^3 + x^2 - x + c$
b. $6x^2 + 2$
c. $\frac{3}{2}x^3 + 2x^2 - x + c$
d. $6x^2 + 2 + c$

120. Calculate $\int 3x^2 e^{x^3} \ dx$
a. $x^3 e^{x^3} + c$
b. $e^{x^3} + c$
c. $x^3 e^{\frac{x^4}{4}} + c$
d. $\ln x^3 + c$

121. Find the area A of the finite region between the graphs of $y = -x + 2$ and $y = x^2 - 4$.
- a. 18
- b. $\dfrac{125}{6}$
- c. $\dfrac{45}{2}$
- d. 25

122. The velocity of a car which starts at position 0 at time 0 is given by the equation $v(t) = 12t - t^2$ for $0 \leq t \leq 12$. Find the position of the car when its acceleration is 0.
- a. 18
- b. 36
- c. 144
- d. 288

123. Which of these graphs is **NOT** representative of the data set shown below?

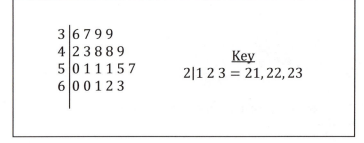

```
3 | 6 7 9 9
4 | 2 3 8 8 9          Key
5 | 0 1 1 1 5 7    2|1 2 3 = 21, 22, 23
6 | 0 0 1 2 3
```

a.

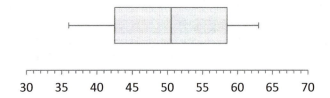

30   35   40   45   50   55   60   65   70

b.

Frequency

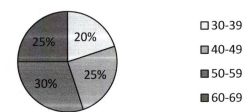

- 30-39
- 40-49
- 50-59
- 60-69

c.

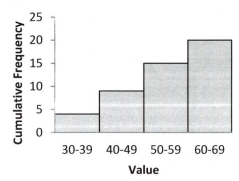

d. All of these graphs represent the data set.

124. Which of these would best illustrate change over time?
   a. Pie chart
   b. Line graph
   c. Box-and-whisker plot
   d. Venn diagram

125. Which of these is the least biased sampling technique?
   a. To assess his effectiveness in the classroom, a teacher distributes a teacher evaluation to all of his students. Responses are anonymous and voluntary.
   b. To determine the average intelligence quotient (IQ) of students in her school of 2,000 students, a principal uses a random number generator to select 300 students by student identification number and has them participate in a standardized IQ test.
   c. To determine which video game is most popular among his fellow eleventh graders at school, a student surveys all of the students in his English class.
   d. Sixty percent of students at the school have a parent who is a member of the Parent-Teacher Association (PTA). To determine parent opinions regarding school improvement programs, the Parent-Teacher Association (PTA) requires submission of a survey response with membership dues.

126. Which of these tables properly displays the measures of central tendency which can be used for nominal, interval, and ordinal data?

a.

	Mean	Median	Mode
Nominal			x
Interval	x	x	x
Ordinal		x	x

b.

	Mean	Median	Mode
Nominal			x
Interval	x	x	x
Ordinal	x	x	x

c.

	Mean	Median	Mode
Nominal	x	x	x
Interval	x	x	x
Ordinal	x	x	x

d.

	Mean	Median	Mode
Nominal			x
Interval	x	x	
Ordinal	x	x	x

Use the following data to answer questions 127-129:

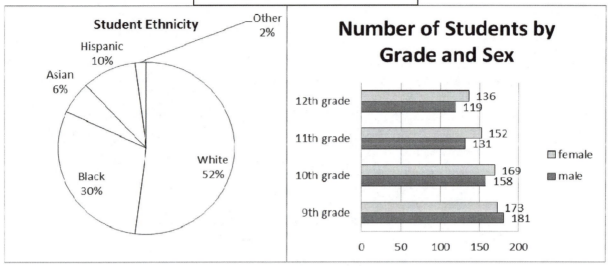

127. Which of these is the greatest quantity?
   a. The average number of male students in the 11th and 12th grades
   b. The number of Hispanic students at the school
   c. The difference in the number of male and female students at the school
   d. The difference in the number of 9th and 12th grader students at the school

128. Compare the two quantities.

<u>Quantity A</u>

The percentage of white students at the school, rounded to the nearest whole number

<u>Quantity B</u>

The percentage of female students at the school, rounded to the nearest whole number

   a. Quantity A is greater.
   b. Quantity B is greater.
   c. The two quantities are the same.
   d. The relationship cannot be determined from the given information.

129. An eleventh grader is chosen at random to represent the school at a conference. What is the approximate probability that the student is male?
   a. 0.03
   b. 0.11
   c. 0.22
   d. 0.46

The box-and-whisker plot displays student test scores by class period. Use the data to answer questions 130 through 132:

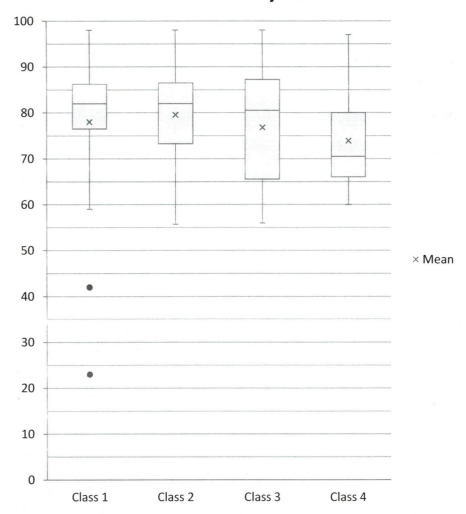

130. Which class has the greatest range of test scores?
    a. Class 1
    b. Class 2
    c. Class 3
    d. Class 4

131. What is the probability that a student chosen at random from class 2 made above a 73 on this test?
    a. 0.25
    b. 0.5
    c. 0.6
    d. 0.75

132. Which of the following statements is true of the data?
   a. The mean better reflects student performance in class 1 than the median.
   b. The mean test score for class 1 and 2 is the same.
   c. The median test score for class 1 and 2 is the same.
   d. The median test score is above the mean for class 4.

133. In order to analyze the real estate market for two different zip codes within the city, a realtor examines the most recent 100 home sales in each zip code. She considered a house which sold within the first month of its listing to have a market time of one month; likewise, she considered a house to have a market time of two months if it sold after having been on the market for one month but by the end of the second month. Using this definition of market time, she determined the frequency of sales by number of months on the market. The results are displayed below.

Which of the following is a true statement for these data?

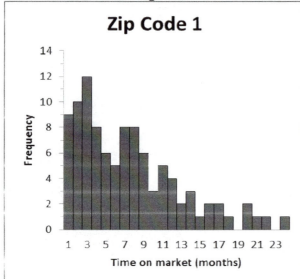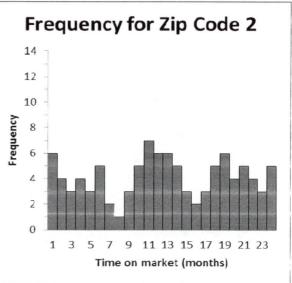

   a. The median time a house spends on the market in Zip Code 1 is five months less than Zip Code 2
   b. On average, a house spent seven months longer on the market in Zip Code 2 than in Zip Code 1.
   c. The mode time on the market is higher for Zip Code 1 than for Zip Code 2.
   d. The median time on the market is less than the mean time on the market for Zip Code 1.

134. Attending a summer camp are 12 six-year-olds, 15 seven-year-olds, 14 eight-year-olds, 12 nine-year-olds, and 10 ten-year-olds. If a camper is randomly selected to participate in a special event, what is the probability that he or she is at least eight years old?
   a. $\frac{2}{9}$

   b. $\frac{22}{63}$

   c. $\frac{4}{7}$

   d. $\frac{3}{7}$

135. A small company is divided into three departments as shown. Two individuals are chosen at random to attend a conference. What is the approximate probability that two women from the same department will be chosen?

	Department 1	Department 2	Department 3
Women	12	28	16
Men	18	14	15

    a. 8.6%
    b. 10.7%
    c. 11.2%
    d. 13.8%

136. A random sample of students at an elementary school were asked these three questions:

Do you like carrots?
Do you like broccoli?
Do you like cauliflower?

The results of the survey are shown below. If these data are representative of the population of students at the school, which of these is most probable?

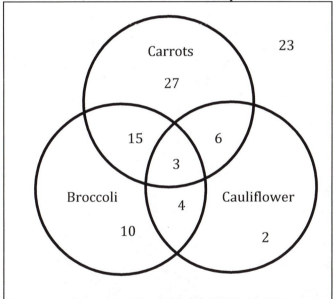

    a. A student chosen at random likes broccoli.
    b. If a student chosen at random likes carrots, he also likes at least one other vegetable.
    c. If a student chosen at random likes cauliflower and broccoli, he also likes carrots.
    d. A student chosen at random does not like carrots, broccoli, or cauliflower.

Use the information below to answer questions 137 and 138:

Each day for 100 days, a student tossed a single misshapen coin three times in succession and recorded the number of times the coin landed on heads. The results of his experiment are shown below.

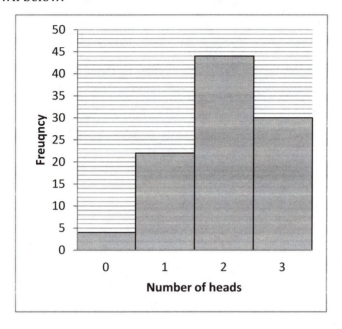

137. Given these experimental data, which of these approximates P(heads) for a single flip of this coin.
    a. 0.22
    b. 0.5
    c. 0.67
    d. 0.74

138. Which of these shows the graphs of the probability distributions from ten flips of this misshapen coin and ten flips of a fair coin?

a.

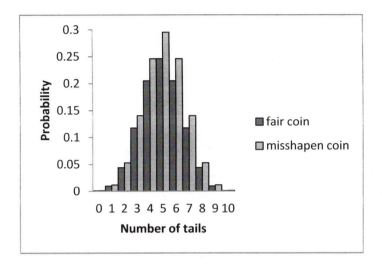

b.

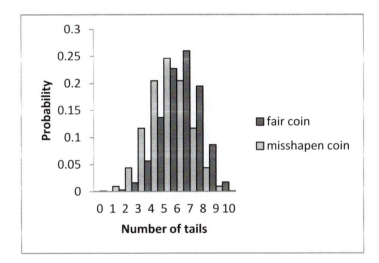

c.

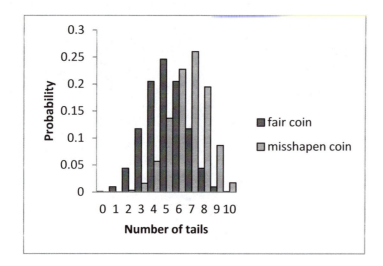

d.

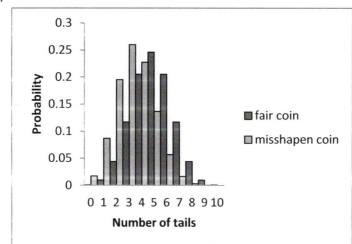

139. Which of these does **NOT** simulate randomly selecting a student from a group of 11 students?
    a. Assigning each student a unique card value of A, 1, 2, 3, 4, 5, 6, 7, 8, 9, or J, removing queens and kings from a standard deck of 52 cards, shuffling the remaining cards, and drawing a single card from the deck
    b. Assigning each student a unique number 0-10 and using a computer to randomly generate a number within that range
    c. Assigning each student a unique number from 2 to 12 ; rolling two dice and finding the sum of the numbers on the dice
    d. All of these can be used as a simulation of the event.

140. Gene P has three possible alleles, or gene forms, called a, b and c. Each individual carries two copies of Gene P, one of which is inherited from his or her mother and the other of which is inherited from his or her father. If the two copies of Gene P are of the same form, the individual is homozygous for that allele; otherwise, the individual is heterozygous. A simulation is performed to determine the genotypes, or genetic make-ups, of 500 individuals selected at random from the population. 500 two-digit numbers are generator using a random number generator. Based on the relative frequencies of each allele, the digit 0 is assigned to represent allele a, the digits 1 and 2 to represent allele b, and the digits 3-9 to represent allele c.

```
28 93 97 37 92 00 27 21 87 13 62 62 15 31 55 09 47 07 54 88 38 88 10 98 34 01 45 14 34 46
38 61 93 22 37 39 57 03 93 50 53 16 28 65 81 60 21 12 13 10 19 91 04 18 49 01 99 30 11 16
00 48 04 63 59 24 02 42 23 06 32 52 19 18 94 94 46 63 87 41 79 39 85 20 43 20 15 03 39 33
77 45 66 77 70 92 25 27 68 71 89 35 98 55 85 47 60 97 12 92 53 44 45 41 51 22 09 23 81 33
04 35 43 48 32 80 36 95 64 56 34 74 55 37 64 84 51 50 25 99 51 94 19 46 10 44 17 25 75 52
47 35 70 65 08 50 98 09 02 24 30 59 00 03 21 40 30 86 16 53 91 28 17 97 58 75 76 73 83 54
40 54 13 38 36 67 74 80 63 12 41 27 96 61 66 05 60 69 96 15 56 82 57 31 83 26 24 78 42 76
49 56 06 57 78 67 02 96 40 82 29 14 07 29 62 90 31 08 26 71 61 18 22 84 23 33 49 29 90 07
08 05 14 59 72 86 44 69 68 99 06 11 95 43 72 58 28 93 97 37 92 00 27 21 87 13 62 62 15 31
55 09 47 07 54 88 38 88 10 98 34 01 45 14 34 46 38 61 93 22 37 39 57 03 93 50 53 16 28 65
81 60 21 12 13 10 19 91 04 18 49 01 99 30 11 16 00 48 04 63 59 24 02 42 23 06 32 52 19 18
94 94 46 63 87 41 79 39 85 20 43 20 15 03 39 33 77 45 66 77 70 92 25 27 68 71 89 35 98 55
85 47 60 97 12 92 53 44 45 41 51 22 09 23 81 33 04 35 43 48 32 80 36 95 64 56 34 74 55 37
64 84 51 50 25 99 51 94 19 46 10 44 17 25 75 52 47 35 70 65 08 50 98 09 02 24 30 59 00 03
21 40 30 86 16 53 91 28 17 97 58 75 76 73 83 54 40 54 13 38 36 67 74 80 63 12 41 27 96 61
66 05 60 69 96 15 56 82 57 31 83 26 24 78 42 76 49 56 06 57 78 67 02 96 40 82 29 14 07 29
62 90 31 08 26 71 61 18 22 84 23 33 49 29 90 07 08 05 14 59
```

Using the experimental probability that an individual will be homozygous for allele a or for allele b, predict the number of individuals in a population of 100,000 who will be homozygous for either allele.
   a. 2,800
   b. 5,000
   c. 5,400
   d. 9,000

141. The intelligence quotients (IQs) of a randomly selected group of 300 people are normally distributed with a mean IQ of 100 and a standard deviation of 15. In a normal distribution, approximately 68% of values are within one standard deviation of the mean. About how many individuals from the selected group have IQs of at least 85?
   a. 96
   b. 200
   c. 216
   d. 252

142. How many different seven-digit telephone numbers can be created in which no digit repeats and in which zero cannot be the first digit?
   a. 5,040
   b. 35,280
   c. 544,320
   d. 3, 265,920

- 47 -

143. A teacher wishes to divide her class of twenty students into four groups, each of which will have three boys and two girls. How many possible groups can she form?

    a. 248

    b. 6,160

    c. 73,920

    d. 95,040

144. In how many distinguishable ways can a family of five be seated a circular table with five chairs if Tasha and Mac must be kept separated?

    a. 6

    b. 12

    c. 24

    d. 60

145. Which of these defines the recursive sequence $a_1 = -1, a_{n+1} = a_n + 2$ explicitly?

    a. $a_n = 2n - 3$

    b. $a_n = -n + 2$

    c. $a_n = n - 2$

    d. $a_n = -2n + 3$

146. What is the sum of the series 200+100+50+25+ ...?

    a. 300

    b. 400

    c. 600

    d. The sum is infinite.

147. For vector $v = (4, 3)$ and vector $w = (-3,4)$, find $2(v + w)$.

    a. $(2, 14)$

    b. $(14, -2)$

    c. $(1,7)$

    d. $(7, -1)$

148. Simplify $\begin{bmatrix} 2 & 0 & -5 \end{bmatrix} \left(\begin{bmatrix} 4 \\ 2 \\ -1 \end{bmatrix} - \begin{bmatrix} 3 \\ 5 \\ -5 \end{bmatrix} \right)$.

    a. $[-18]$

    b. $\begin{bmatrix} 2 \\ 0 \\ -20 \end{bmatrix}$

    c. $\begin{bmatrix} 2 & 0 & -20 \end{bmatrix}$

    d. $\begin{bmatrix} 2 & 0 & -5 \\ -6 & 0 & 15 \\ 8 & 0 & -20 \end{bmatrix}$

149. Consider three sets, of which one contains the set of even integers, one contains the factors of twelve, and one contains elements 1, 2, 4, and 9. If each set is assigned the name A, B, or C, and $A \cap B \subseteq B \cap C$, which of these must be set C?

    a. The set of even integers

    b. The set of factors of 12

    c. The set {1, 2, 4, 9}

    d. The answer cannot be determined from the given information.

150. Last year, Jenny tutored students in math, in chemistry, and for the ACT. She tutored ten students in math, eight students in chemistry, and seven students for the ACT. She tutored five students in both math and chemistry, and she tutored four students both in chemistry and for the ACT, and five students both in math and for the ACT. She tutored three students in all three subjects. How many students did Jenny tutor last year?

    a. 34
    b. 25
    c. 23
    d. 14

Answers and Explanations

1. C: Because drawing a dodecagon and counting its diagonals is an arduous task, it is useful to employ a different problem-solving strategy. One such strategy is to draw polygons with fewer sides and look for a pattern in the number of the polygons' diagonals.

(triangle)	3	0
(square)	4	2
(pentagon)	5	5
(hexagon)	6	9
Heptagon	7	14
Octagon	8	20

A quadrilateral has two more diagonals than a triangle, a pentagon has three more diagonals than a quadrilateral, and a hexagon has four more diagonals than a pentagon. Continue this pattern to find that a dodecagon has 54 diagonals.

2. B: The problem does not give any information about the size of the bracelet or the spacing between any of the charms. Nevertheless, creating a simple illustration which shows the order of the charms will help when approaching this problem. For example, the circle below represents the bracelet, and the dotted line between A and B represents the clasp. On the right, the line shows the stretched out bracelet and possible positions of charms C, D, and E based on the parameters.

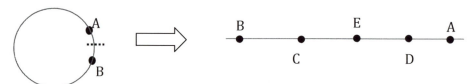

From the drawing above, it appears that statement I is true, but it is not necessarily so. The alternative drawing below also shows the charms ordered correctly, but the distance between B and E is now less than that between D and A.

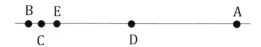

Statement II must be true: charm E must lie between B and D. Statement III must also be true: the distance between charms E and D must be less than that between C and A, which includes charms E and D in the space between them.

3. B: The population is approximately 36,000, so one quarter of the population consists of about 9,000 individuals under age 35. A third of 9,000 is 3,000, the approximate number of students in grades K-12. Since there are thirteen grades, there are about 230 students in each grade. So, the number of fourth graders is between 200 and 300.

4. A: The final sales price of the rug is $1.08(0.7 \cdot \$296) = \$223.78$ at Store A, $1.08(\$220 - \$10) = \$226.80$ at Store B, and $\$198 + \$35 = \$233$ at Store C.

5. C: The expression representing the monthly charge for Company A is $\$25 + \$0.05m$, where m is the time in minutes spent talking on the phone. Set this expression equal to the monthly charge for Company B, which is $50. Solve for m to find the number of minutes for which the two companies charge the same amount:

$$\$25 + \$0.05m = \$50$$
$$\$0.05m = \$25$$
$$m = 500$$

Notice that the answer choices are given in hours, not in minutes. Since there are 60 minutes in an hour, $m = \frac{500}{60}$ hours = $8\frac{1}{3}$ hours. One-third of an hour is twenty minutes, so m = 8 hours, 20 minutes.

6. D: When the dress is marked down by 20%, the cost of the dress is 80% of its original price; thus, the reduced price of the dress can be written as $\frac{80}{100}x$, or $\frac{4}{5}x$, where x is the original price. When discounted an extra 25%, the dress costs 75% of the reduced price, or $\frac{75}{100}\left(\frac{4}{5}x\right)$, or $\frac{3}{4}\left(\frac{4}{5}x\right)$, which simplifies to $\frac{3}{5}x$. So the final price of the dress is three-fifths of the original price.

7. D: Since there are 100 cm in a meter, on a 1:100 scale drawing, each centimeter represents one meter. Therefore, an area of one square centimeter on the drawing represents one square meter in actuality. Since the area of the room in the scale drawing is 30 cm^2, the room's actual area is 30 m^2.

Another way to determine the area of the room is to write and solve an equation, such as this one:
$$\frac{l}{100} \cdot \frac{w}{100} = 30 \text{ cm}^2 \text{ , where } l \text{ and } w \text{ are the dimensions of the actual room}$$
$$\frac{lw}{1000} = 30 \text{ cm}^2$$
$$lw = 300{,}000 \text{ cm}^2$$
$$\text{Area} = 300{,}000 \text{ cm}^2$$

Since this is not one of the answer choices, convert cm^2 to m^2: $300{,}000 \text{ cm}^2 \cdot \frac{1 \text{ m}}{100 \text{ cm}} \cdot \frac{1 \text{ m}}{100 \text{ cm}} = 30 \text{ m}^2$.

8. C: Since the ratio of wages and benefits to other costs is 2:3, the amount of money spent on wages and benefits is $\frac{2}{5}$ of the business's total expenditure. $\frac{2}{5} \cdot \$130{,}000 = \$52{,}000$.

9. A: The height of the ball is a function of time, so the equation can be expressed as $f(t) = -16t^2 + 64t + 5$, and the average rate of change can be found by calculating $\frac{f(3)-f(1)}{3-1}$.

$$\frac{-16(3)^2 + 64(3) + 5 - [-16(1)^2 + 64(1) + 5]}{2} = \frac{-144 + 192 + 5 - (-16 + 64 + 5)}{2} = \frac{0}{2} = 0$$

Alternatively, the rate of change can be determined by finding the slope of the secant line through points $(1, f(1))$ and $(3, f(3))$. Notice that this is a horizontal line, which has a slope of 0.

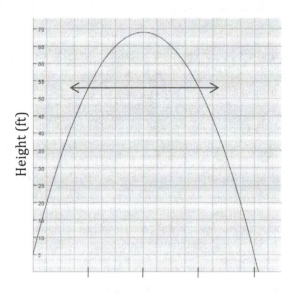

Time (sec)

10. B: Since rate in mph $= \frac{\text{distance in miles}}{\text{time in hours}}$, Zeke's driving speed on the way to Atlanta and home from Atlanta in mph can be expressed as d/3 and d/2, respectively, when d=distance between Zeke's house and his destination . Since Zeke drove 20 mph faster on his way home, $\frac{d}{2} - \frac{d}{3} = 20$.

$$6\left(\frac{d}{2} - \frac{d}{3} = 20\right)$$
$$3d - 2d = 120$$
$$d = 120$$

Since the distance between Zeke's house and the store in Atlanta is 120 miles, Zeke drove a total distance of 240 miles in five hours. Therefore, his average speed was $\frac{240 \text{ miles}}{5 \text{ hours}} = 48$ mph.

11. C: Aaron ran four miles from home and then back again, so he ran a total of eight miles. Therefore, statement III is false. Statements I and II, however, are both true. Since Aaron ran eight miles in eighty minutes, he ran an average of one mile every ten minutes, or six miles per hour; he ran two miles from point A to B in 20 minutes and four miles from D to E in 40 minutes, so his running speed between both sets of points was the same.

12. D: First, use the table to determine the values of $(a * b)$ and $(c * d)$.

*	a	b	c	d
a	d	a	b	c
b	a	b	c	d
c	b	c	d	a
d	c	d	a	b

$(a * b) = a$ and $(c * d) = a$, so $(a * b) * (c * d) = a * a$, which is equal to d.

13. B: When $y = x^3$, $x = \sqrt[3]{y}$. Similarly, when $y = e^x$, $x = \ln y$ for $y > 0$. On the other hand, when $y = x + a$, $x = y - a$; when $y = 1/x$, $x = 1/y$ for $x, y \neq 0$; and when $y = \sin x$, $x = \sin^{-1} y$.

14. B: Deductive reasoning moves from one or more general statements to a specific, while inductive reasoning makes a general conclusion based on a series of specific instances or observations. Whenever the premises used in deductive reasoning are true, the conclusion drawn is necessarily true. In inductive reasoning, it is possible for the premises to be true and the conclusion to be false since there may exist an exception to the general conclusion drawn from the observations made.

15. A: The first argument's reasoning is valid, and since its premises are true, the argument is also sound. The second argument's reasoning is invalid; that the premises are true is irrelevant. (For example, consider the true premises "all cats are mammals" and "all dogs are mammals;" it cannot be logically concluded that all dogs are cats.) The third argument's reasoning is valid, but since one of its premises is false, the argument is not sound.

16. C: The logical representation $p \rightarrow q$ means that p implies q. In other words, if p, then q. Unlike the contrapositive (Choice C), neither the converse (choice A) nor the inverse (choice B) is necessarily true. For example, consider this statement: all cats are mammals. This can be written as an if/then statement: if an animal is a cat, then the animal is a mammal. The converse would read, "If an animal is a mammal, then the animal is a cat;" of course, this is not necessarily true since there are many mammals other than cats. The inverse statement, "If an animal is not a cat, then the animal is not a mammal," is false. The contrapositive, "If an animal is not a mammal, then the animal is not a cat" is true since there are no cats which are not mammals.

17. D: The symbol $\wedge$ is the logical conjunction symbol. In order for statement $(p \wedge q)$ to be true, both statements p and q must be true. The $\sim$ symbol means "not," so if $(p \wedge q)$ is true, then $\sim(p \wedge q)$ is false, and if $(p \wedge q)$ is false, then $\sim(p \wedge q)$ is true. The statement $q \leftrightarrow \sim(p \wedge q)$ is true when the value of q is the same as the value of $\sim(p \wedge q)$.

p	q	$(p \wedge q)$	$\sim(p \wedge q)$	$q \leftrightarrow \sim(p \wedge q)$
T	T	T	F	F
T	F	F	T	F
F	T	F	T	T
F	F	F	T	F

18. D: The value "0" means "false," and the value "1" means "true." For the logical disjunction "or," the output value is true if either or both input values are true, else it is false. For the logical conjunction "and," the output value is true only if both input values are true. "Not A" is true when A is false and is false when A is true.

X	Y	Z	not Y	not Z	not Y or not Z	X and (not Y or not Z)
0	0	0	1	1	1	0
0	0	1	1	0	1	0
0	1	0	0	1	1	0
0	1	1	0	0	0	0
1	0	0	1	1	1	1
1	0	1	1	0	1	1
1	1	0	0	1	1	1
1	1	1	0	0	0	0

19. A: The Babylonians used a base-60 numeral system, which is still used in the division of an hour into 60 minutes, a minute into 60 seconds, and a circle into 360 degrees. (The word "algebra" and its development as a discipline separate from geometry are attributed to the Arabic/Islamic civilization. The Greek philosopher Thales is credited with using deductive reasoning to prove geometric concepts. Boolean logic and algebra was introduced by British mathematician George Boole.)

20. C: Leonhard Euler made many important contributions to the field of mathematics. One such contribution, Euler's formula $e^{i\varphi} = \cos\varphi + i\sin\varphi = 0$, can be written as $e^{i\pi} + 1 = 0$ when $\varphi = \pi$. This identity is considered both mathematically remarkable and beautiful, as it links together five important mathematical constants, $e, i, \pi, 0$ and 1.

21. B: The notation $\mathbb{P} \subseteq \mathbb{N} \subseteq \mathbb{Z} \subseteq \mathbb{Q} \subseteq \mathbb{R} \subseteq \mathbb{C}$ means that the set of prime numbers is a subset of the set natural numbers, which is a subset of the set of integers, which is a subset of the set of rational numbers, which is a subset of the set real numbers, which is a subset of the set of complex numbers.

22. A: The set of whole numbers, $\{0, 1, 2, 3, \ldots\}$, does not contain the number -4. Since -4 is an integer, it is also a rational number and a real number.

23. D: In order for a set to be a group under operation $*$,
   1. The set must be closed under that operation. In other words, when the operation is performed on any two members of the set, the result must also be a member of that set.
   2. The set must demonstrate associativity under the operation: $a * (b * c) = (a * b) * c$
   3. There must exist an identity element e in the group: $a * e = e * a = a$
   4. For every element in the group, there must exist an inverse element in the group: $a * b = b * a = e$

Note: the group need not be commutative for every pair of elements in the group. If the group demonstrates commutativity, it is called an abelian group.

The set of prime numbers under addition is not closed. For example, 3+5=8, and 8 is not a member of the set of prime numbers. Similarly, the set of negative integers under multiplication is not closed since the product of two negative integers is a positive integer. Though the set of negative integers under addition is closed and is associative, there exists no identity element (the number zero in this case) in the group. The set of positive rational numbers under multiplication is closed and associative; the multiplicative identity 1 is a member of the group, and for each element in the group, there is a multiplicative inverse (reciprocal).

24. A: First, multiply the numerator and denominator by the denominator's conjugate, $4 + 2i$. Then, simplify the result and write the answer in the form $a + bi$.

$$\frac{2 + 3i}{4 - 2i} \cdot \frac{4 + 2i}{4 + 2i} = \frac{8 + 4i + 12i + 6i^2}{16 - 4i^2} = \frac{8 + 16i - 6}{16 + 4} = \frac{2 + 16i}{20} = \frac{1}{10} + \frac{4}{5}i$$

- 54 -

25. D: First, simplify the expression within the absolute value symbol.
$$|(2 - 3i)^2 - (1 - 4i)|$$
$$|4 - 12i + 9i^2 - 1 + 4i|$$
$$|4 - 12i - 9 - 1 + 4i|$$
$$|-6 - 8i|$$
The absolute value of a complex number is its distance from 0 on the complex plane. Use the Pythagorean Theorem (or the 3-4-5 Pythagorean triple and similarity) to find the distance of $-6 - 8i$ from the origin.

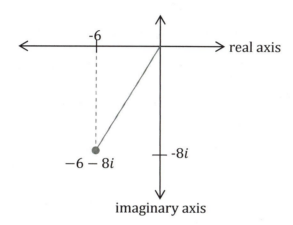

Since the distance from the origin to the point $-6 - 8i$ is 10, $|-6 - 8i| = 10$.

26. B: In order for a set to be a group under operation $*$,
1. The set must be closed under that operation. In other words, when the operation is performed on any two members of the set, the result must also be a member of that set.
2. The set must demonstrate associativity under the operation: $a * (b * c) = (a * b) * c$
3. There must exist an identity element e in the group: $a * e = e * a = a$
4. For every element in the group, there must exist an inverse element in the group: $a * b = b * a = e$

Choice A can easily be eliminated as the correct answer because the set $\{-i, 0, i\}$ does not contain the multiplicative identity 1. Though choices C and D contain the element 1, neither is closed: for example, since $i \cdot i = -1$, -1 must be an element of the group. Choice B is closed, contains the multiplicative identity 1, and the inverse of each element is included in the set as well. Of course, multiplication is an associative operation, so the set $\{-1, 1, i, -i\}$ forms a group under multiplication

×	-1	1	i	-i
-1	1	-1	-i	i
1	-1	1	i	-i
i	-i	i	-1	1
-i	i	-i	1	-1

27. D: The identity element is d since $d\#a = a\#d = a, d\#b = b\#d = b, d\#c = c\#d = c$, and $d\#d = d$. The inverse of element c is c since $c\#c = d$, the identity element. The operation # is commutative because $a\#b = b\#a, a\#c = c\#a$, etc. Rather than check that the operation is commutative for each pair of elements, note that elements in the table display symmetry about the diagonal elements; this indicates that the operation is indeed commutative.

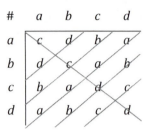

28. C: "The square of twice the sum of x and three is equal to the product of twenty-four and x" is represented by the equation $[2(x + 3)]^2 = 24x$. Solve for x.
$$[2(x + 3)]^2 = 24x$$
$$[2x + 6]^2 = 24x$$
$$4x^2 + 24x + 36 = 24x$$
$$4x^2 = -36$$
$$x^2 = -9$$
$$x = \pm\sqrt{-9}$$
$$x = \pm 3i$$

So, $-3i$ is a possible value of x.

29. C: If x is a prime number and that the greatest common factor of x and y is greater than 1, the greatest common factor of x and y must be x. The least common multiple of two numbers is equal to the product of those numbers divided by their greatest common factor. So, the least common multiple of x and y is $\frac{xy}{x} = y$. Therefore, the values in the two columns are the same.

30. D: Since a and b are even integers, each can be expressed as the product of 2 and an integer. So, if we write $a = 2x$ and $b = 2y$, $3(2x)^2 + 9(2y)^3 = c$.
$$3(4x^2) + 9(8y^3) = c$$
$$12x^2 + 72y^3 = c$$
$$12(x^2 + 6y^3) = c$$

Since c is the product of 12 and some other integer, 12 must be a factor of c. Incidentally, the numbers 2, 3, and 6 must also be factors of c since each is also a factor of 12.

31. C: Choice C is the equation for the greatest integer function. A function is a relationship in which for every element of the domain (x), there is exactly one element of the range (y). Graphically, a relationship between x and y can be identified as a function if the graph passes the vertical line test.

The first relation is a parabola on its side, which fails the vertical line test for functions. A circle (Choice B) also fails the vertical line test and is therefore not a function. The relation in Choice D pairs two elements of the range with one of the elements of the domain, so it is also not a function.

32. B: The area of a triangle is $A = \frac{1}{2}bh$, where b and h are the lengths of the triangle's base and height, respectively. The base of the given triangle is x, but the height is not given. Since the triangle is a right triangle and the hypotenuse is given, the triangle's height can be found using the Pythagorean Theorem.

$$x^2 + h^2 = 6^2$$
$$h = \sqrt{36 - x^2}$$

To find the area of the triangle in terms of x, substitute $\sqrt{36 - x^2}$ for the height and x for the base of the triangle into the area formula.

$$A = \frac{1}{2}bh$$
$$A(x) = \frac{1}{2}(x)(\sqrt{36 - x^2})$$
$$A(x) = \frac{x\sqrt{36 - x^2}}{2}$$

33. A: $[g \circ f]x = g(f(x)) = g(2x + 4) = (2x + 4)^2 - 3(2x + 4) + 2 = 4x^2 + 16x + 16 - 6x - 12 + 2 = 4x^2 + 10x + 6$.

34. C: One way to approach the problem is to use the table of values to first write equations for $f(x)$ and $g(x)$: $f(x) = 2x^2$ and $g(x) = 2x + 5$. Then, use those equations to find $f(g(-4))$.

$$g(-4) = 2(-4) + 5 = -3$$
$$f(-3) = 2(-3)^2 = 18$$

So, $f(g(-4)) = 18$.

35. D: By definition, when $f(x)$ and $g(x)$ are inverse functions, $f(g(x)) = g(f(x)) = x$. So, $f(g(4)) = 4$.

36. B: To find the inverse of an equation, solve for x in terms of y; then, exchange the variables x and y. Or, to determine if two functions $f(x)$ and $g(x)$ are inverses, find $f(g(x))$ and $g(f(x))$; if both results are x, then $f(x)$ and $g(x)$ are inverse functions.

For example, to find the inverse of $y = x + 6$, rewrite the equation $x = y + 6$ and solve for y. Since $y = x - 6$, the two given equations given in Choice A are inverses. Likewise, to find the inverse of $y = \frac{2x+3}{x-1}$, rewrite the equation as $x = \frac{2y+3}{y-1}$ and solve for y:

$$xy - x = 2y + 3$$
$$xy - 2y = x + 3$$
$$y(x - 2) = x + 3$$
$$y = \frac{x + 3}{x - 2}$$

The two equations given in Choice C are inverses.

Here, the second method is used to determine if the two equations given in Choices B and D are inverses: Choice B: $y = 2(2x + 3) - 3 = 4x + 6$. The two given equations are **NOT** inverses. Choice D: $y = \frac{(2x+1)-1}{2} = \frac{2x}{2} = x$ and $y = 2\left(\frac{x-1}{2}\right) + 1 = x - 1 + 1 = x$, so the two given equations are inverses.

37. A: Below is the graph of $g(x)$.

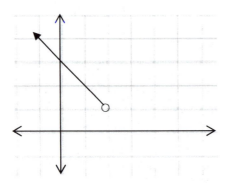

Statement II is true: the graph is indeed discontinuous at $x = 2$. Since $g(3) = 2(3) - 1 = 5$, Statement I is false, and since the range is $y > 1$, Statement III is also false.

38. A: In the range $(-\infty, -1)$, the graph represented is $y = x^2$. In the range $[-1, 2)$, the graph is the greatest integer function, $y = [\![x]\!]$. In the range $[-2, \infty)$, the graph is $y = -2x + 6$.

39. B: If $y = a(x + b)(x + c)^2$, the degree of the polynomial is 3. Since the degree of the polynomial is odd and the leading coefficient is positive $(a > 0)$, the end behavior of the graph is below.

$$\swarrow \ \nearrow$$

Therefore, neither Choice A nor Choice C can be a graph of $y = a(x + b)(x + c)^2$. The maximum number of "bumps" (or critical points) in the graph is at most one less than the degree of the polynomial, so Choice D, which has three bumps, cannot be the graph of the function. Choice B displays the correct end behavior and has two bumps, so it is a possible graph of $y = a(x + b)(x + c)^2$.

40. B: $5n + 3s \geq 300$ when $n =$ number of non-student tickets which must be sold and $s =$ number of student tickets which must be sold. The intercepts of this linear inequality are $n = 60$ and $s = 100$. The solid line through the two intercepts represents the minimum number of each type of ticket which must be sold in order to offset production costs. All points above the line represent sales which result in a profit for the school.

41. D: The vertex form of a quadratic equation is $y = a(x - h)^2 + k$, where $x = h$ is the parabola's axis of symmetry and (h, k) is the parabola's vertex. The vertex of the graph is (-1,3), so the equation can be written as $y = a(x + 1)^2 + 3$. The parabola passes through point (1,1), so $1 = a(1 + 1)^2 + 3$. Solve for a:
$$1 = a(1 + 1)^2 + 3$$
$$1 = a(2)^2 + 3$$
$$1 = 4a + 3$$
$$-2 = 4a$$
$$-\frac{1}{2} = a$$

- 58 -

So, the vertex form of the parabola is $y = -\frac{1}{2}(x+1)^2 + 3$. Write the equation in the form $y = ax^2 + bx + c$.

$$y = -\frac{1}{2}(x+1)^2 + 3$$
$$y = -\frac{1}{2}(x^2 + 2x + 1) + 3$$
$$y = -\frac{1}{2}x^2 - x - \frac{1}{2} + 3$$
$$y = -\frac{1}{2}x^2 - x + \frac{5}{2}$$

42. D: There are many ways to solve quadratic equations in the form $ax^2 + bx + c = 0$; however, some methods, such as graphing and factoring, may not be useful for some equations, such as those with irrational or complex roots. Solve this equation by completing the square or by using the Quadratic Formula, $x = \frac{-b \pm \sqrt{b^2 - 4ac}}{2a}$.

$$7x^2 + 6x + 2 = 0; a = 7, b = 6, c = 2$$

$$x = \frac{-b \pm \sqrt{b^2 - 4ac}}{2a}$$
$$x = \frac{-6 \pm \sqrt{6^2 - 4(7)(2)}}{2(7)}$$
$$x = \frac{-6 \pm \sqrt{36 - 56}}{14}$$
$$x = \frac{-6 \pm \sqrt{-20}}{14}$$
$$x = \frac{-6 \pm 2i\sqrt{5}}{14}$$
$$x = \frac{-3 \pm i\sqrt{5}}{7}$$

43. C: A system of linear equations can be solved by using matrices or by using the graphing, substitution, or elimination (also called linear combination) method. The elimination method is shown here:
$$3x + 4y = 2$$
$$2x + 6y = -2$$
In order to eliminate x by linear combination, multiply the top equation by 2 and the bottom equation by −3 so that the coefficients of the x-terms will be additive inverses.
$$2(3x + 4y = 2)$$
$$-3(2x + 6y = -2)$$
Then, add the two equations and solve for y.
$$6x + 8y = 4$$
$$\underline{-6x - 18y = 6}$$
$$-10y = 10$$
$$y = -1$$

Substitute -1 for y in either of the given equations and solve for x.
$$3x + 4(-1) = 2$$
$$3x - 4 = 2$$
$$3x = 6$$
$$x = 2$$
The solution to the system of equations is $(2, -1)$.

44. C: The graph below shows that the lines are parallel and that the shaded regions do not overlap. There is no solution to the set of inequalities given in Choice C.

$6x + 2y \leq 12$
$2y \leq -6x + 12$
$y \leq -3x + 6$

$3x \geq 8 - y$
$y \geq -3x + 8$

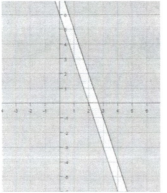

As in Choice C, the two lines given in Choice A are parallel; however, the shading overlaps between the lines, so that region represents the solution to the system of inequalities.

The shaded regions for the two lines in Choice B do not overlap except at the boundary, but since the boundary is same, the solution to the system of inequalities is the line $y = -2x + 6$.

Choice D contains a set of inequalities which have intersecting shaded regions; the intersection represents the solution to the system of inequalities.

45. A: First, write three equations from the information given in the problem. Since the total number of tickets sold was 810, $x + y + z = 810$. The ticket sales generated $14,500, so $15x + 25y + 20z = 14,500$. The number of children under ten was the same as twice the number of adults and seniors, so $x = 2(y + z)$, which can be rewritten as $x - 2y - 2z = 0$.

The coefficients of each equation are arranged in the rows of a 3x3 matrix, which, when multiplied by the 3x1 matrix arranging the variables x, y, and z, will give the 3x1 matrix which arranges the constants of the equations.

46. B: There are many ways to solve this system of equations. One is shown below.
1. Multiply the second equation by 2 and combine it with the first equation to eliminate the variable y.

$$2x - 4y + z = 10$$
$$\underline{-6x + 4y - 8z = -14}$$
$$-4x \qquad - 7z = -4$$

2. Multiply the third equation by –2 and combine it with the original second equation to eliminate y.

$$-3x + 2y - 4z = -7$$
$$\underline{-2x - 2y + 6z = 2}$$
$$-5x \qquad + 2z = -5$$

3. Multiply the equation from step one by 5 and the equation from step two by -4 and combine to eliminate x.

$$-20x - 35z = -20$$
$$\underline{20x - 8z = 20}$$
$$-43z = 0$$
$$z = 0$$

4. Substitute 0 for z in the equation from step 2 to find x.

$$-5x + 2(0) = -5$$
$$-5x = -5$$
$$x = 1$$

5. Substitute 0 for z and 1 for x into the first original equation to find y.

$$2(1) - 4y + (0) = 10$$
$$2 - 4y = 10$$

$$-4y = 8$$
$$y = -2$$

47. B: One way to solve the equation is to write $x^4 + 64 = 20x^2$ in the quadratic form $(x^2)^2 - 20(x^2) + 64 = 0$. This trinomial can be factored as $(x^2 - 4)(x^2 - 16) = 0$. In each set of parentheses is a difference of squares, which can be factored further: $(x + 2)(x - 2)(x + 4)(x - 4) = 0$. Use the zero product propery to find the solutions to the equation.

$$
\begin{array}{cccc}
x + 2 = 0 & x - 2 = 0 & x + 4 = 0 & x - 4 = 0 \\
x = -2 & x = 2 & x = -4 & x = 4
\end{array}
$$

48. A: First, set the equation equal to zero.

$$3x^3y^2 - 45x^2y = 15x^3y - 9x^2y^2$$
$$3x^3y^2 - 15x^3y + 9x^2y^2 - 45x^2y = 0$$

Then, factor the equation.

$$3x^2y(xy - 5x + 3y - 15) = 0$$
$$3x^2y[x(y - 5) + 3(y - 5)] = 0$$
$$3x^2y[(y - 5)(x + 3)] = 0$$

Use the zero product property to find the solutions.

$$
\begin{array}{ccc}
3x^2y = 0 & y - 5 = 0 & x + 3 = 0 \\
x = 0 & y = 5 & x = -3 \\
y = 0 & &
\end{array}
$$

So, the solutions are $x = \{0, -3\}$ and $y = \{0,5\}$.

49. D: The degree of $f(x)$ is 1, the degree of $g(x)$ is 2, and the degree of $h(x)$ is 3. The leading coefficient for each function is 2. Functions $f(x)$ and $h(x)$ have exactly one real zero ($x = 1$), while $g(x)$ has two real zeros ($x = \pm 1$):

$f(x)$	$g(x)$	$h(x)$
$0 = 2x - 2$	$0 = 2x^2 - 2$	$0 = 2x^3 - 2$
$-2x = -2$	$-2x^2 = -2$	$-2x^3 = -2$
$x = 1$	$x^2 = 1$	$x^3 = 1$
	$x = 1; \; x = -1$	$x = 1$

50. B: The path of a bullet is a parabola, which is the graph of a quadratic function. The path of a sound wave can be modeled by a sine or cosine function. The distance an object travels over time given a constant rate is a linear relationship, while radioactive decay is modeled by an exponential function.

51. B: First, use the properties of logarithms to rewrite $2 \log_4 y + \log_4 16 = 3$.
- Since $N \log_a M = \log_a M^N$, $2 \log_4 y = \log_4 y^2$. Replacing $2 \log_4 y$ by its equivalent in the given equation gives $\log_4 y^2 + \log_4 16 = 3$.
- Since $\log_a M + \log_a N = \log_a MN$, $\log_4 y^2 + \log_4 16 = \log_4 16\, y^2$. Thus, $\log_4 16\, y^2 = 3$.
- Since $\log_a M = N$ is equivalent to $a^N = M$, $\log_4 16\, y^2 = 3$ is equivalent to $4^3 = 16y^2$.

Then, solve for y. (Note that y must be greater than zero.)
$$4^3 = 16y^2$$
$$64 = 16y^2$$
$$4 = y^2$$
$$2 = y$$
Finally, substitute 2 for y in the expression $\log_y 256$ and simplify: $\log_2 256 = 8$ since $2^8 = 256$.

52. B: First, apply the laws of exponents to simplify the expression on the left.
$$\frac{(x^2y)(2xy^{-2})^3}{16x^5y^2} + \frac{3}{xy}$$

$$\frac{(x^2y)(8x^3y^{-6})}{16x^5y^2} + \frac{3}{xy}$$

$$\frac{8x^5y^{-5}}{16x^5y^2} + \frac{3}{xy}$$

$$\frac{1}{2y^7} + \frac{3}{xy}$$

Then, add the two fractions.

$$\frac{1}{2y^7} \cdot \frac{x}{x} + \frac{3}{xy} \cdot \frac{2y^6}{2y^6}$$

$$\frac{x}{2xy^7} + \frac{6y^6}{2xy^7}$$

$$\frac{x + 6y^6}{2xy^7}$$

53. C: If $f(x) = 10^x$ and $f(x) = 5$, then $5 = 10^x$. Since $\log_{10}x$ is the inverse of 10^x, $\log_{10}5 = \log_{10}(10^x) = x$. Therefore, $0.7 \approx x$.

54. C: The graph shown is the exponential function $y = 2^x$. Notice that the graph passes through (-2, 0.25), (0,1), (2,4).

	Choice A	Choice B	Choice C	Choice D
x	x^2	$\sqrt{x}$	2^x	$\log_2 x$
-2	4	undefined in $\mathbb{R}$	0.25	undefined
0	0	0	1	undefined
2	4	$\sqrt{2}$	4	1

55. C: The x-intercept is the point at which $f(x) = 0$. When $0 = \log_b x$, $b^0 = x$; since $b^0 = 1$, the x-intercept of $f(x) = \log_b x$ is always 1. If $f(x) = \log_b x$ and $x = b$, then $f(x) = \log_b b$, which is, by definition, 1. $(b^1 = b.)$ If $g(x) = b^x$, then $f(x)$ and g(x) are inverse functions and are therefore symmetric with respect to $y = x$. The statement choice C is not necessarily true since $x < 1$ includes numbers less than or equal to zero, the values for which the function is undefined. The statement $f(x) < 0$ is true only for x values between 0 and 1 $(0 < x < 1)$.

56. D: Bacterial growth is exponential. Let x be the number of doubling times and a be the number of bacteria in the colony originally transferred into the broth and y be the number of bacteria in the broth after a doubling times.

Time	Number of doubling times (x)	$a(2^x)$	Number of bacteria (y)
0	0	$a(2^0) = a$	1×10^6
20 minutes	1	$a(2^1)$	2×10^6
40 minutes	2	$a(2^2)$	4×10^6
60 minutes	3	$a(2^3)$	$\mathbf{8 \times 10^6}$

Determine how many bacteria were present in the original colony. Either work backwards by halving the number of bacteria (see gray arrows above) or calculate a:
$$a(2^3) = 8 \times 10^6$$
$$8a = 8 \times 10^6$$
$$a = 10^6$$
The equation for determining the number of bacteria is $y = (2^x) \cdot 10^6$. Since the bacteria double every twenty minutes, they go through three doubling times every hour. So, when the bacteria are allowed to grow for eight hours, they will have gone through 24 doubling times. When $x = 24$, $y = (2^{24}) \cdot 10^6 = 16777216 \times 10^6$, which is approximately 1.7×10^{13}.

57. C: Since the pH scale is a base–10 logarithmic scale, a difference in pH of 1 indicates a ratio between strengths of 10. So, an acid with a pH of 3 is 100 times stronger than an acid with a pH of 5.

58. A:

$$\sqrt{\frac{-28x^6}{27y^5}} = \frac{2x^3 i\sqrt{7}}{3y^2\sqrt{3y}} \cdot \frac{\sqrt{3y}}{\sqrt{3y}} = \frac{2x^3 i\sqrt{21y}}{9y^2}$$

59. C:

$-4 \le 2 + 3(x-1) \le 2$	$-2x^2 + 2 \ge x^2 - 1$	$\dfrac{11 - |3x|}{7} \ge 2$	$3|2x| + 4 \le 10$
$-6 \le 3(x-1) \le 0$	$-3x^2 \ge -3$	$11 - |3x| \ge 14$	$3|2x| \le 6$
$-2 \le x - 1 \le 0$	$x^2 \le 1$	$-|3x| \ge 3$	$|2x| \le 2$
$-1 \le x \le 1$	$-1 \le x \le 1$	$|3x| \le -1$	$-2 \le 2x \le 2$
		No solution	$-1 \le x \le 1$

60. D: When solving radical equations, check for extraneous solutions.

$2 - \sqrt{x} = \sqrt{x - 20}$
$\left(2 - \sqrt{x}\right)^2 = \sqrt{x - 20}^2$
$4 - 4\sqrt{x} + x = x - 20$
$-4\sqrt{x} = -24$
$\sqrt{x} = 6$
$\sqrt{x}^2 = 6^2$
$x = 36$

$2 - \sqrt{36} = \sqrt{36 - 20}$
$2 - 6 = \sqrt{16}$
$-4 \ne 4$

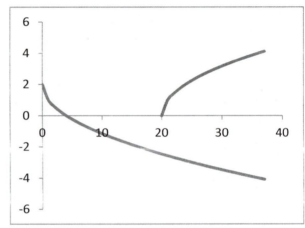

Since the solution does not check, there is no solution. Notice that the graphs $y = 2 - \sqrt{x}$ and $y = \sqrt{x - 20}$ do not intersect, which confirms there is no solution.

61. B: Notice that choice C cannot be correct since $x \ne 1$. ($x = 1$ results in a zero in the denominator.)

$$\frac{x-2}{x-1} = \frac{x-1}{x+1} + \frac{2}{x-1}$$
$$(x-1)(x+1)\left(\frac{x-2}{x-1} = \frac{x-1}{x+1} + \frac{2}{x-1}\right)$$
$$(x+1)(x-2) = (x-1)^2 + 2(x+1)$$
$$x^2 - x - 2 = x^2 - 2x + 1 + 2x + 2$$
$$x^2 - x - 2 = x^2 + 3$$
$$-x = 5$$
$$x = -5$$

- 64 -

62. A: The denominator of a fraction cannot equal zero. Therefore, for choices A and B,.

$$x^2 - x - 2 \neq 0$$
$$(x + 1)(x - 2) \neq 0$$
$$x + 1 \neq 0 \quad x - 2 \neq 0$$
$$x \neq -1 \quad x \neq 2.$$

Since choice A is in its simplest form, there are vertical asymptotes at $x = -1$ and $x = 2$. However, for choice B,

$$\frac{3x + 3}{x^2 - x - 2} = \frac{3(x + 1)}{(x + 1)(x - 2)} = \frac{3}{x - 2}.$$

So, at $x = -2$ there is an asymptote, while at $x = -1$, there is simply a hole in the graph. So, choice B does not match the given graph. For choice C, there are asymptotes at $x = -1$ and $x = 2$; however, notice that it is possible for the graph of choice C to intersect the x-axis since it is possible that $y = 0$ (when $x = 0.5$). Since the given graph does not have an x-intercept, choice C is incorrect. For choice A, it is not possible that y=0, so it is a possible answer. Check a few points on the graph to make sure they satisfy the equation.

x	y
-2	$\frac{3}{4}$
0	$-\frac{3}{2}$
$\frac{1}{2}$	$-\frac{4}{3}$
1	$-\frac{3}{2}$
3	$\frac{3}{4}$

The points $\left(-2, \frac{3}{4}\right), \left(0, -\frac{3}{2}\right), \left(\frac{1}{2}, -\frac{4}{3}\right), \left(1, -\frac{3}{2}\right),$ and $\left(3, \frac{3}{4}\right)$ are indeed points on the graph.

63. A: An easy way to determine which is the graph of $f(x) = -2|-x + 4| - 1$ is to find $f(x)$ for a few values of x. For example, $f(x) = -2|0 + 4| - 1 = -9$. Graphs A and B pass through $(0, -9)$, but graphs C and D do not. $f(4) = -2|-4 + 4| - 1 = -1$. Graphs A and D pass through $(4, -1)$, but graphs B and C do not. Graph A is the correct graph. $f(x) = -2|-x + 4| - 1$ shifts the graph of $y = |x|$ to the left four units, reflects it across the y-axis, inverts it, makes it narrower, and shifts it down one unit.

64. C: The first function shifts the graph of $y = \frac{1}{x}$ to the right one unit and up one unit. The domain and range of $y = \frac{1}{x}$ are $\{x : x \neq 0\}$ and $\{y : y \neq 0\}$, so the domain and range of $y = \frac{1}{x-1} + 1$ are $\{x : x \neq 1\}$ and $\{y : y \neq 1\}$. The element 1 is not in its domain.

The second function inverts the graph of $y = \sqrt{x}$ and shifts it to the left two units and down one unit. The domain and range of $y = \sqrt{x}$ are $\{x : x \geq 0\}$ and $\{y : y \geq 0\}$, so the domain and range of $y = -\sqrt{x + 2} - 1$ are $\{x : x \geq -2\}$ and $\{y : y \leq -1\}$. The range does not contain the element 2.

The third function shifts the graph of $y = |x|$ to the left two units and down three units. The domain of $y = |x|$ the set of all real numbers and range is $\{y: y \geq 0\}$, so the domain of $y = |x + 2| - 3$ is the set of all real numbers and the range is $\{y: y \geq -3\}$. The domain contains the element 1 and the range contains the element 2.

This is the graph of the fourth function. The domain of this piece-wise function is the set of all real numbers, and the range is $\{y: y \leq -1\}$. The range does not contain the element 2.

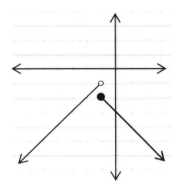

65. B: First, state the exclusions of the domain.
$$x^3 + 2x^2 - x - 2 \neq 0$$
$$(x + 2)(x - 1)(x + 1) \neq 0$$
$$x + 2 \neq 0 \quad x - 1 \neq 0 \quad x + 1 \neq 0$$
$$x \neq -2 \quad x \neq 1 \quad x \neq -1$$

To determine whether there are asymptotes or holes at these values of x, simplify the expression $\frac{x^2 - x - 6}{x^3 + 2x^2 - x - 2}$.

$$\frac{(x - 3)(x + 2)}{(x + 2)(x - 1)(x + 1)} = \frac{x - 3}{(x - 1)(x + 1)}$$

There are asymptotes at $x = 1$ and at $x = -1$ and a hole at $x = 2$. Statement I is false.

To find the x-intercept of $f(x)$, solve $f(x) = 0$. $f(x) = 0$ when the numerator is equal to zero. The numerator equals zero when $x = 2$ and $x = 3$; however, 2 is excluded from the domain of $f(x)$, so the x-intercept is 3. To find the y-intercept of $f(x)$, find $f(0)$. $\frac{0^2 - 0 - 6}{0^3 + 2(0)^2 - 0 - 2} = \frac{-6}{-2} = 3$. The y-intercept is 3. Statement II is true.

66. C: The period of the pendulum is a function of the square root of the length of its string, and is independent of the mass of the pendulum or the angle from which it is released. If the period of Pendulum 2's swing is four times the period of Pendulum 1's swing, then the length of Pendulum 1's string must be 16 times the length of Pendulum 2's swing since all other values besides L in the expression $2\pi\sqrt{\frac{L}{g}}$ remain the same.

67. D: There are many ways Josephine may have applied her knowledge to determine how to approximately measure her medicine using her plastic spoon. The only choice which correctly uses dimensional analysis is choice D: the dosage ≈ 25 cc $\cdot \frac{1 \text{ ml}}{1 \text{ cc}} \cdot \frac{1 \text{L}}{1000 \text{ml}} \cdot \frac{0.5 \text{ gal}}{2 \text{L}} \cdot \frac{16 \text{c}}{1 \text{ gal}} \cdot \frac{48t}{1 \text{c}} \cdot \frac{1 \text{ spoonful}}{1t} \rightarrow \frac{25}{1000} \cdot \frac{1}{4} \cdot$ $16 \cdot 48 \approx 5$.

- 66 -

68. C: If 1" represents 60 feet, 10" represents 600 ft, which is the same as 200 yards.

69. D: If the distance between the two houses is 10 cm on the map, then the actual distance between the houses is 100 m.

To find x, use the Pythagorean Theorem:
$x^2 + (x + 20)^2 = (100)^2$
$x^2 + x^2 + 40x + 400 = 10000$
$2x^2 + 40x - 9600 = 0$
$2(x^2 + 20x - 4800) = 0$
$2(x - 60)(x + 80) = 0$
$x = 60 \quad x = -80$

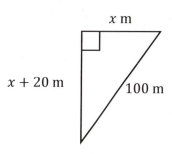

Since x represents a distance, it cannot equal –80. Since $x = 60$, $20 = 80$. Roxana walks a total of 140 m to get to her friend's house.

70. D: $\triangle ABC$ is similar to the smaller triangle with which it shares vertex A. $AB = (2x - 1) + (x + 7) = 3x + 6$. $AC = 4 + 8 = 12$. Set up a proportion and solve for x:
$$\frac{3x + 6}{12} = \frac{2x - 1}{4}$$
$$12x + 24 = 24x - 12$$
$$36 = 12x$$
$$3 = x$$

So, $AB = 3x + 6 = 3(3) + 6 = 15$.

71. B: Percent error $= \frac{|\text{actual value} - \text{measured value}|}{\text{actual value}} \times 100\%$, and the average percent error is the sum of the percent errors for each trial divided by the number of trials.

	% error Trial 1	% error Trial 2	% error Trial 3	% error Trial 4	Average percent error
Scale 1	0.1%	0.2%	0.2%	0.1%	0.15%
Scale 2	2.06%	2.09%	2.10%	2.08%	2.08%

The percent error for Scale 1 is less than the percent error for Scale 2, so it is more accurate. The more precise scale is Scale 2 because its range of values, 10.210 g $-$ 10.206 g $=$ 0.004 g, is smaller than the Scale 2's range of values, 10.02 g $-$ 9.98 g $=$ 0.04 g.

72. C: If l and w represent the length and width of the enclosed area, its perimeter is equal to $2l + 2w$; since the fence is positioned x feet from the lot's edges on each side, the perimeter of the lot is $2(l + 2x) + 2(w + 2x)$. Since the amount of money saved by fencing the smaller are is $432, and since the fencing material costs $12 per linear foot, 36 fewer feet of material are used to fence around the playground than would have been used to fence around the lot. This can be expressed as the equation $2(l + 2x) + 2(w + 2x) - (2l + 2w) = 36$.

$$2(l + 2x) + 2(w + 2x) - (2l + 2w) = 36$$
$$2l + 4x + 2w + 4x - 2l - 2w = 36$$
$$8x = 36$$
$$x = 4.5 \text{ ft}$$

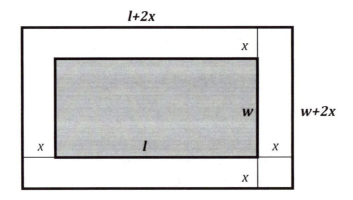

The difference in the area of the lot and the enclosed space is 141 yd^2, which is the same as 1269 ft^2. So, $(l + 2x)(w + 2x) - lw = 1269$. Substituting 4.5 for x,

$$(l + 9)(w + 9) - lw = 1269$$
$$lw + 9l + 9w + 81 - lw = 1269$$
$$9l + 9w = 1188$$
$$9(l + w) = 1188$$
$$l + w = 132 \text{ ft}$$

Therefore, the perimeter of the enclosed space, $2(l + w)$, is $2(132) = 264$ ft. The cost of 264 ft of fencing is $264 \cdot \$12 = \$3,168$.

73. B: The volume of Natasha's tent is $\frac{x^2 h}{3}$. If she were to increase by 1 ft the length of each side of the square base, the tent's volume would be $\frac{(x+1)^2 h}{3} = \frac{(x^2+2x+1)(h)}{3} = \frac{x^2 h + 2xh + h}{3} = \frac{x^2 h}{3} + \frac{2xh + h}{3}$. Notice this is the volume of Natasha's tent, $\frac{x^2 h}{3}$, increased by $\frac{2xh + h}{3}$, or $\frac{h(2x+1)}{3}$.

74. A: The area of a circle is πr^2, so the area of a semicircle is $\frac{\pi r^2}{2}$. Illustrated below is a method which can be used to find the area of the shaded region.

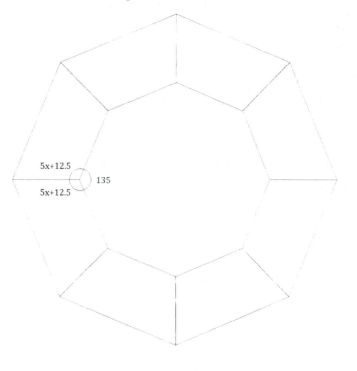

$$r = 6x$$
$$A = \frac{\pi(6x)^2}{2}$$

$$r = 5x$$
$$-\quad \frac{\pi(5x)^2}{2}$$

$$r = 4x$$
$$+\quad \frac{\pi(4x)^2}{2}$$

$$r = 3x$$
$$-\quad \frac{\pi(3x)^2}{2}$$

$$r = 2x$$
$$+\quad \frac{\pi(2x)^2}{2}$$

$$r = x$$
$$-\quad \frac{\pi(x)^2}{2}$$

The area of the shaded region is $\frac{\pi(36x^2-25x^2+16x^2-9x^2+4x^3-x^2)}{2} = \frac{(21x^2)\pi}{2}$.

75. B. Euclidean geometry is based on the flat plane. One of Euclid's five axioms, from which all Euclidean geometric theorems are derived, is the parallel postulate, which states that in a plane, for any line l and point A not on l, exactly one line which passes through A does not intersect l.

Non-Euclidean geometry considers lines on surfaces which are not flat. For instance, on the Earth's surface, if point A represents the North Pole and line l represents the equator (which does not pass through A), all lines of longitude pass through point A and intersect line l. In elliptical geometry, there are infinitely many lines which pass though A and intersect l, and there is no line which passes through A which does not also intersect l. In hyperbolic geometry, the opposite is true. When A is not on l, all lines which pass through A diverge from l, so none of the lines through A intersect l.

76. B: When four congruent isosceles trapezoids are arranged in an arch, the bases of the trapezoid come together to form regular octagons, the smaller of which is shown to the right. The measure of each angle of a regular octagon is 135°. $\left(\frac{(8-2)(180°)}{8} = 135°.\right)$ From the relationship of two of the trapezoid's base angles with one of the octagon's interior angles, write and solve an equation:

$(5x + 12.5) + (5x + 12.5) + 135 = 360$
$10x + 160 = 360$
$10x = 200$
$x = 20$

77. C: Sketch a diagram (this one is not to scale) and label the known segments. Use the property that two segments are congruent when they originate from the same point outside of a circle and are tangent to the circle.

The point of tangency of $\overline{CB}$ divides the segment into two pieces measuring 4 and 6; the point of tangency of $\overline{BA}$ divides the segment into two pieces measuring 6 and 8; the point of tangency of $\overline{AD}$ divides the segment into two pieces measuring 8 and 4. Therefore $AD = 8 + 4 = 12$.

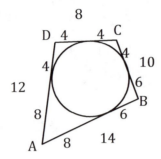

78. D: Let b represent the base of the triangle. The height h of the triangle is the altitude drawn from the vertex opposite of b to side b.

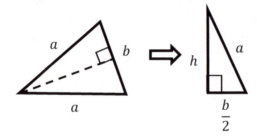

The height of the triangle can be found in terms of a and b by using the Pythagorean theorem:

$$h^2 + \left(\frac{b}{2}\right)^2 = a^2$$

$$h = \sqrt{a^2 - \frac{b^2}{4}} = \sqrt{\frac{4a^2 - b^2}{4}} = \frac{\sqrt{4a^2 - b^2}}{2}$$

The area of a triangle is $A = \frac{1}{2}bh$, so $A = \frac{1}{2}b\left(\frac{\sqrt{4a^2-b^2}}{2}\right) = \frac{b\sqrt{4a^2-b^2}}{4}$.

79. B: Since ∠ADC is a right triangle with legs measuring 5 and 12, its hypotenuse measures 13. (5-12-13 is a Pythagorean triple.)

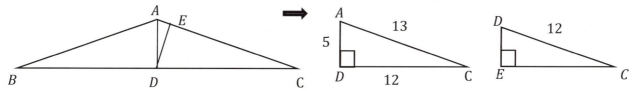

∠ADC and ∠DEC are both right triangles which share vertex C. By the AA similarity theorem ∠ADC~∠DEC. Therefore, a proportion can be written and solved to find DE.

$$\frac{5}{DE} = \frac{13}{12}$$
$$DE = 4.6$$

80. C: The center of the sphere is shared by the center of the cube, and each of the corners of the cube touches the surface of the sphere. Therefore, the diameter of the sphere is the line which passes through the center of the cube and connects one corner of the cube to the opposite corner on the opposite face. Notice in the illustration below that the diameter d of the sphere can be represented as the hypotenuse of a right triangle with a short leg measuring 4 units. (Since the volume of the cube is 64 cubic units, each of its sides measures $\sqrt[3]{64} = 4$ units.) The long leg of the triangle is the diagonal of the base of the cube. Its length can be found using the Pythagorean theorem: $4^2 + 4^2 = x^2$; $x = \sqrt{32} = 4\sqrt{2}$.

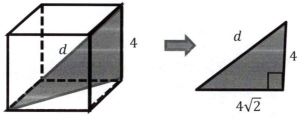

Use the Pythagorean theorem again to find d, the diameter of the sphere: $d^2 = \left(4\sqrt{2}\right)^2 + 4^2$; $d = \sqrt{48} = 4\sqrt{3}$. To find the volume of the sphere, use the formula $V = \frac{4}{3}\pi r^3$. Since the radius r of the sphere is half the diameter, $r = 2\sqrt{3}$, and $V = \frac{4}{3}\pi(2\sqrt{3})^3 = \frac{4}{3}\pi\left(24\sqrt{3}\right) = 32\pi\sqrt{3}$ cubic units.

81. D. Since it is given that $\overline{FD} \cong \overline{BC}$ and $\overline{AB} \cong \overline{DE}$, step 2 needs to establish either that $\overline{AC} \cong \overline{EF}$ or that $\triangle ABC \cong \triangle FDE$ in order for step 5 to show that $\triangle ABC \cong \triangle EDF$. The statement $\overline{AC} \cong \overline{EF}$ cannot be shown directly from the given information. On the other hand, $\triangle ABC \cong \triangle FDE$ can be determined: when two parallel lines ($\overline{BC} \| \overline{FG}$) are cut by a transversal ($\overline{AE}$), alternate exterior angles ($\triangle ABC, \triangle FDE$) are congruent. Therefore, $\triangle ABC \cong \triangle EDF$ by the side-angle-side (SAS) theorem.

82. A: Step 5 established that $\triangle ABC \cong \triangle EDF$. Because corresponding parts of congruent triangles are congruent (CPCTC), $\angle BAC \cong \angle DEF$. This is useful to establish when trying to prove $\overline{FE}\|\overline{AG}$: when two lines ($\overline{FE}$ and $\overline{AG}$) are cut by a transversal ($\overline{AE}$) and alternate interior angles ($\angle BAC, \angle DEF$) are congruent, then the lines are parallel. The completed proof is shown immediately following.

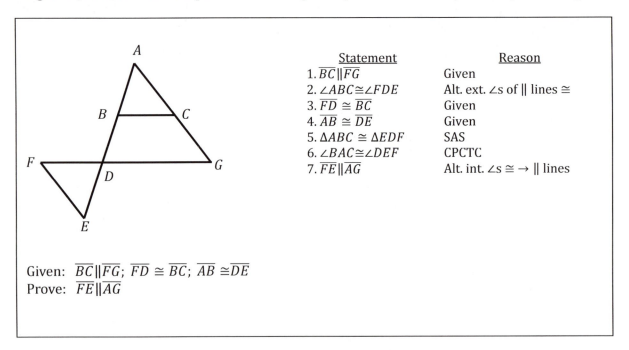

	Statement	Reason
1.	$\overline{BC}\|\overline{FG}$	Given
2.	$\angle ABC \cong \angle FDE$	Alt. ext. $\angle$s of $\|$ lines $\cong$
3.	$\overline{FD} \cong \overline{BC}$	Given
4.	$\overline{AB} \cong \overline{DE}$	Given
5.	$\triangle ABC \cong \triangle EDF$	SAS
6.	$\angle BAC \cong \angle DEF$	CPCTC
7.	$\overline{FE}\|\overline{AG}$	Alt. int. $\angle$s $\cong \rightarrow \|$ lines

Given: $\overline{BC}\|\overline{FG}$; $\overline{FD} \cong \overline{BC}$; $\overline{AB} \cong \overline{DE}$
Prove: $\overline{FE}\|\overline{AG}$

83. B: A cube has six square faces. The arrangement of these faces in a two-dimensional figure is a net of a cube if the figure can be folded to form a cube. Figures A, C, and D represent three of the eleven possible nets of a cube. If choice B is folded, however, the bottom square in the second column will overlap the fourth square in the top row, so the figure does not represent a net of a cube.

84. D: The cross-section is a hexagon.

85. A: Use the formula for the volume of a sphere to find the radius of the sphere:

$$V = \frac{4}{3}\pi r^3$$
$$36\pi = \frac{4}{3}\pi r^3$$
$$36 = \frac{4}{3}r^3$$
$$36 = \frac{4}{3}r^3$$
$$27 = r^3$$
$$3 = r$$

Then, substitute the point $(h, k, l) = (1, 0, -2)$ and the radius $r = 3$ into the equation of a sphere:

$$(x - h)^2 + (y - k)^2 + (z - l)^2 = r^2$$
$$(x - 1)^2 + y^2 + (z + 2)^2 = 3^2$$
$$(x - 1)^2 + y^2 + (z + 2)^2 = 9$$
$$x^2 - 2x + 1 + y^2 + z^2 + 4z + 4 = 9$$
$$x^2 + y^2 + z^2 - 2x + 4z = 4$$

86. B: The triangle is a right triangle with legs 3 and 4 units long.

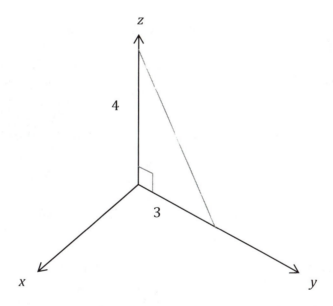

If the triangle is rotated about the z-axis, the solid formed is a cone with a height of 4 and a radius of 3; this cone has volume $V = \frac{1}{3}\pi r^2 h = \frac{1}{3}\pi 3^2 4 = 12\pi$ cubic units. If the triangle is rotated about the y-axis, the solid formed is a cone with a height of 3 and a radius of 4. This cone has volume $V = \frac{1}{3}\pi r^2 h = \frac{1}{3}\pi 4^2 3 = 16\pi$ cubic units. The difference in the volumes of the two cones is $16\pi - 12\pi = 4\pi$ cubic units.

87. D: The point $(5, -5)$ lies on the line which has a slope of -2 and which passes through $(3, -1)$. If $(5, -5)$ is one of the endpoints of the line, the other would be $(1,3)$.

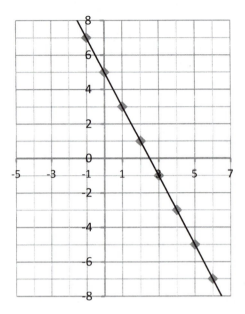

88. D: Since all of the answer choices are parallelograms, determine whether the parallelogram is also a rhombus or a rectangle or both. One way to do this is by examining the parallelogram's diagonals. If the parallelogram's diagonals are perpendicular, then the parallelogram is a rhombus. If the parallelogram's diagonals are congruent, then the parallelogram is a rectangle. If a parallelogram is both a rhombus and a rectangle, then it is a square.

To determine whether the diagonals are perpendicular, find the slopes of the diagonals of the quadrilateral:
- Diagonal 1: $\frac{6-2}{-5-3} = \frac{4}{-8} = -\frac{1}{2}$
- Diagonal 2: $\frac{0-8}{-3-1} = -\frac{8}{-4} = 2$

The diagonals have opposite inverse slopes and are therefore perpendicular. Thus, the parallelogram is a rhombus.

To determine whether the diagonals are congruent, find the lengths of the diagonals of the quadrilateral:
- Diagonal 1: $\sqrt{(6-2)^2 + (-5-3)^2} = \sqrt{(4)^2 + (-8)^2} = \sqrt{16 + 64} = \sqrt{80} = 4\sqrt{5}$
- Diagonal 2: $\sqrt{(0-8)^2 + (-3-1)^2} = \sqrt{(-8)^2 + (-4)^2} = \sqrt{64 + 16} = \sqrt{80} = 4\sqrt{5}$

The diagonals are congruent, so the parallelogram is a rectangle.

Since the polygon is a rhombus and a rectangle, it is also a square.

89. A: The equation of the circle is given in general form. When the equation is written in the standard form $(x - h)^2 + (y - k)^2 = r^2$, where (h, k) is the center of the circle and r is the radius of the circle, the radius is easy to determine. Putting the equation into standard form requires completing the square for x and y:

$$x^2 - 10x + y^2 + 8y = -29$$
$$(x^2 - 10x + 25) + (y^2 + 8y + 16) = -29 + 25 + 16$$
$$(x - 5)^2 + (y + 4)^2 = 12$$

Since $r^2 = 12,$ and since r must be a positive number, $r = \sqrt{12} = 2\sqrt{3}.$

90. D: One way to determine whether the equation represents an ellipse, a circle, a parabola, or a hyperbola is to find the determinant $b^2 - 4ac$ of the general equation form of a conic section, $ax^2 + bxy + cy^2 + dx + ey + f = 0$, where $a, b, c, d, e,$ and f are constants. Given that the conic section is non-degenerate, if the determinant is positive, then the equation is a hyperbola; if the determinant is negative, then the equation is a circle (when $a = c$ and $b = 0$) or an ellipse; and if the determinant is zero, then the equation is a parabola. For $2x^2 - 3y^2 - 12x + 6y - 15 = 0, a = 2,\ b = 0,\ c = -3,\ d = -12,$ $e = 6,$ and $f = -15$. The determinant $b^2 - 4ac$ is equal to $0^2 - 4(2)(-3) = 24.$ Since the determinant is positive, the graph is hyperbolic.

Another way to determine the shape of the graph is to look at the coefficients for the x^2 and y^2 terms in the given equation. If one of the coefficients is zero (in other words, if there is either an x^2 or a y^2 term in the equation but not both), then the equation is a parabola; if the coefficients have the same sign, then the graph is an ellipse or circle; and if the coefficients have opposite signs, then the graph is a hyperbola. Since the coefficient of x^2 is 2 and the coefficient of y^2 is -3, the graph is a hyperbola. That the equation can be written in the standard form for a hyperbola, $\frac{(x-h)^2}{a^2} - \frac{(y-k)^2}{b^2} = 1$, confirms the conclusion.

$$2x^2 - 3y^2 - 12x + 6y - 15 = 0$$
$$2x^2 - 12x - 3y^2 + 6y = 15$$
$$2(x^2 - 6x) - 3(y^2 - 2y) = 15$$
$$2(x^2 - 6x + 9) - 3(y^2 - 2y + 1) = 15 + 2(9) - 3(1)$$
$$2(x - 3)^2 - 3(y - 1)^2 = 30$$
$$\frac{(x - 3)^2}{15} - \frac{(y - 1)^2}{10} = 1$$

91. B: The graph of $f(x)$ is a parabola with a focus of (a, b) and a directrix of $y = -b$. The axis of symmetry of a parabola passes through the focus and vertex and is perpendicular to the directrix. Since the directrix is a horizontal line, the axis of symmetry is $x = a$; therefore, the x-coordinate of the parabola's vertex must be a. The distance between a point on the parabola and the directrix is equal to the distance between that point and the focus, so the y-coordinate of the vertex must be $y = \frac{-b+b}{2} = 0.$ So, the vertex of the parabola given by $f(x)$ is $(a, 0).$

If $g(x)$ were a translation of $f(x)$, as is the case for choices A, C, and D, the vertices of $f(x)$ and $g(x)$ would differ. Since the vertex of the graph of $g(x)$ is $(a, 0)$, none of those choices represent the correct response. However, if $g(x) = -f(x)$, the vertices of the graphs of both functions would be the same; therefore, this represents a possible relation between the two functions.

92. C: When a figure is reflected twice over non-parallel lines, the resulting transformation is a rotation about the point of intersection of the two lines of reflection. The two lines of reflection $y = x + 2$ and $x = 0$ intersect at (0,2). So, $\Delta A''B''C''$ represents a rotation of ΔABC about the point (0,2). The angle of rotation is equal to twice the angle between the two lines of reflection when measured in a clockwise direction from the first to the second line of reflection. Since the angle between the lines or reflection measures 135°, the angle of rotation which is the composition of the two reflections measures 270°. All of these properties can be visualized by drawing ΔABC, $\Delta A'B'C'$, and $\Delta A''B''C''$.

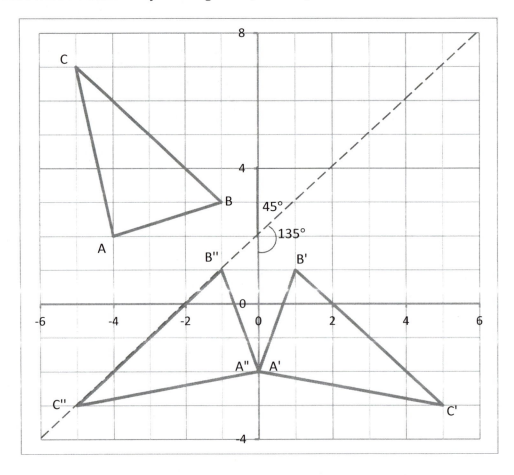

93. B: All regular polygons have rotational symmetry. The angle of rotation is the smallest angle by which the polygon can be rotated such that it maps onto itself; any multiple of this angle will also map the polygon onto itself. The angle of rotation for a regular polygon is the angle formed between two lines drawn from consecutives vertices to the center of the polygon. Since the vertices of a regular polygon lie on a circle, for a regular polygon with n sides, the angle of rotation measures $\frac{360°}{n}$.

Number of sides of regular polygon	Angle of rotation	Angles ≤ 360° which map the polygon onto itself
4	$\frac{360}{4} = 90°$	90°, 180°, 270°, 360°
6	$\frac{360}{6} = 60°$	60°, 120°, 180°, 240°, 300°, 360°
8	$\frac{360}{8} = 45°$	45°, 90°, 135°, 180°, 225°, 270°, 315°, 316°
10	$\frac{360}{10} = 36°$	36°, 72°, 108°, 144°, 180°, 216°, 252°, 288°, 324°, 360°

94. A: Since the y-coordinates of points P and Q are the same, line segment $\overline{PQ}$ is a horizontal line segment whose length is the difference in the x-coordinates a and c. Because the length of a line cannot be negative, and because it is unknown whether $a > c$ or $a < c$, $PQ = |a - c|$ or $|c - a|$. Since the x-coordinates of Q and Q' are the same, line segment $\overline{P'Q}$ is a vertical line segment whose length is $|d - b|$ or $|b - d|$. The quadrilateral formed by the transformation of $\overline{PQ}$ to $\overline{P'Q'}$ is a parallelogram. If the base of the parallelogram is $\overline{PQ}$, then the height is $\overline{P'Q}$ since $\overline{PQ} \perp \overline{P'Q}$. For a parallelogram, $A = bh$, so $A = |a - c| \cdot |b - d|$.

95. B: Since $\tan B = \frac{opposite}{adjacent} = \frac{b}{a}$, choice A is incorrect.

$\cos B = \frac{adjacent}{hypotenuse}$. The hypotenuse of a right triangle is equal to the square root of the sum of the squares of the legs, so $\cos B = \frac{adjacent}{hypotenuse} = \frac{a}{\sqrt{a^2+b^2}}$. Rationalize the denominator: $\frac{a}{\sqrt{a^2+b^2}} \cdot \frac{\sqrt{a^2+b^2}}{\sqrt{a^2+b^2}} = \frac{a\sqrt{a^2+b^2}}{a^2+b^2}$. Choice B is correct.

$\sec B = \frac{hypotenuse}{adjacent} = \frac{\sqrt{a^2+b^2}}{a}$, and $\csc B = \frac{\sqrt{a^2+b^2}}{b}$, so choices C and D are incorrect.

96. C: Find the missing angle measures in the diagram by using angle and triangle properties. Then, use the law of sines to find the distance y between the window and the wife's car: $\frac{60}{\sin 15°} = \frac{y}{\sin 45°}$, so

$y = \frac{60 \sin 45°}{\sin 15} \approx 163.9$ ft. Use this number in a sine or cosine

function to find x: $\sin 30° \approx \frac{x}{163.9}$, so $x \approx 163.9 \sin 30° \approx 82$.

Therefore, the man's wife is parked approximately 82 feet from the building.

Alternatively, notice that when the man is looking down at a 45 degree angle, the triangle that is formed is an isosceles triangle, meaning that the height of his office is the same as the distance the office to his car, or $x + 60$ feet. With this knowledge, the problem can be modeled with a single equation:

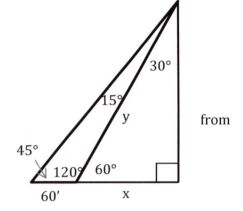

from

$$\frac{x + 60}{x} = \tan 30° \quad or \quad x = \frac{60}{\tan 30° - 1}$$

97. A: The reference angle for $-\frac{2\pi}{3}$ is $2\pi - \frac{2\pi}{3} = \frac{4\pi}{3}$, so $\tan(-\frac{2\pi}{3}) = \tan(\frac{4\pi}{3}) = \frac{\sin(\frac{4\pi}{3})}{\cos(\frac{4\pi}{3})}$. From the unit circle,

the values of $\sin(\frac{4\pi}{3})$ and $\cos(\frac{4\pi}{3})$ are $-\frac{\sqrt{3}}{2}$ and $-\frac{1}{2}$, respectively. Therefore, $\tan(-\frac{2\pi}{3}) = \frac{-\frac{\sqrt{3}}{2}}{-\frac{1}{2}} = \sqrt{3}$.

98. D: On the unit circle, $\sin \theta = \frac{1}{2}$ when $\theta = \frac{\pi}{6}$ and when $\theta = \frac{5\pi}{6}$. Since only $\frac{5\pi}{6}$ is in the given range of

$\frac{\pi}{2} < \theta < \pi, \theta = \frac{5\pi}{6}$.

99. C: Use trigonometric equalities and identities to simplify. $\cos \theta \cot \theta = \cos \theta \cdot \frac{\cos \theta}{\sin \theta} = \frac{\cos^2 \theta}{\sin \theta} = \frac{1 - \sin^2 \theta}{\sin \theta} =$

$\frac{1}{\sin \theta} - \sin \theta = \csc \theta - \sin \theta$.

100. B: The trigonometric identity $\sec^2\theta = \tan^2 \theta + 1$ can be used to rewrite the equation $\sec^2\theta = 2 \tan \theta$ as $\tan^2 \theta + 1 = 2 \tan \theta$, which can then be rearranged into the form $\tan^2 \theta - 2 \tan \theta + 1 = 0$. Solve by factoring and using the zero product property:

$$\tan^2 \theta - 2 \tan \theta + 1 = 0$$
$$(\tan \theta - 1)^2 = 0$$
$$\tan \theta - 1 = 0$$
$$\tan \theta = 1.$$

Since $\tan \theta = 1$ when $\sin \theta = \cos \theta$, for $0 < \theta \leq 2\pi$, $\theta = \frac{\pi}{4}$ or $\frac{5\pi}{4}$.

101. A: Since the graph shows a maximum height of 28 inches above the ground, and since the maximum distance from the road the pebble reaches is when it is at the top of the tire, the diameter of the tire is 28 inches. Therefore, its radius is 14 inches. From the graph, it can be observed that the tire makes 7.5 rotations in 0.5 seconds. Thus, the tire rotates 15 times in 1 second, or $15 \cdot 60 = 900$ times per minute.

102. C: The dashed line represents the sine function (x), and the solid line represents a cosine function $g(x)$. The amplitude of $f(x)$ is 4, and the amplitude of $g(x)$ is 2. The function $y = \sin x$ has a period of 2π, while the graph of function $f(x) = a_1 \sin(b_1 x)$ has a period of 4π; therefore, $b_1 = \frac{2\pi}{4\pi} = 0.5$, which is between 0 and 1. The graph of $g(x) = a_2 \cos(b_2 x)$ has a period of π, so $b_2 = \frac{2\pi}{\pi} = 2$.

103. B: The graph of $f(x)$ is stretched vertically by a factor of 4 with respect to $y = \sin x$, so $a_1 = 4$. The graph of $g(x)$ is stretched vertically by a factor of two and is inverted with respect to the graph of $y = \cos x$, so $a_2 = -2$. Therefore, the statement $a_2 < 0 < a_1$ is true.

104. A: The graph to the right shows the height h in inches of the weight on the spring above the table as a function of time t in seconds. Notice that the height is 3 in above the table at time 0 since the weight was pulled down two inches from its starting position 5 inches above the table. The spring fluctuates 2 inches above and below its equilibrium point, so its maximum height is 7 inches above the table. The graph represents a cosine curve which has been inverted, stretched vertically by a factor of 2, and shifted up five units; also, the graph has been compressed horizontally, with a period of 1 rather than 2π. So, the height of the weight on the spring as a function of time is $h = -2\cos(2\pi t) + 5$.

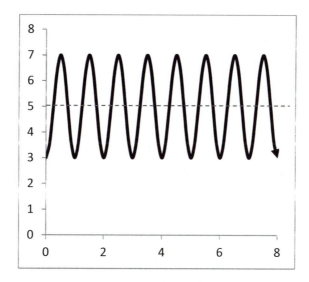

105. C: Since evaluating $\frac{x^3+3x^2-x-3}{x^2-9}$ at $x = -3$ produces a fraction with a zero denominator, simplify the polynomial expression before evaluating the limit:

$$\frac{x^3 + 3x^2 - x - 3}{x^2 - 9} = \frac{x^2(x+3) - 1(x+3)}{(x+3)(x-3)} = \frac{(x+3)(x^2-1)}{(x+3)(x-3)} = \frac{(x+1)(x-1)}{x-3}$$

$$\lim_{x \to -3} \frac{(x+1)(x-1)}{x-3} = \frac{(-3+1)(-3-1)}{-3-3} = \frac{8}{-6} = -\frac{4}{3}.$$

- 79 -

106. B: To evaluate the limit, divide the numerator and denominator by x^2 and use these properties of limits: $\lim_{x \to \infty} \frac{1}{x} = 0$; the limit of a sum of terms is the sum of the limits of the terms; and the limit of a product of terms is the product of the limits of the terms.

$$\lim_{x \to \infty} \frac{x^2 + 2x - 3}{2x^2 + 1} = \lim_{x \to \infty} \frac{\frac{x^2}{x^2} + \frac{2x}{x^2} - \frac{3}{x^2}}{\frac{2x^2}{x^2} + \frac{1}{x^2}} = \lim_{x \to \infty} \frac{1 + \frac{2}{x} - \frac{3}{x^2}}{2 + \frac{1}{x^2}} = \frac{1 + 0 - 0}{2 + 0} = \frac{1}{2}.$$

107. B: Evaluating $\frac{|x-3|}{3-x}$ when $x = 3$ produces a fraction with a zero denominator. To find the limit as x approaches 3 from the right, sketch a graph or make a table of values.

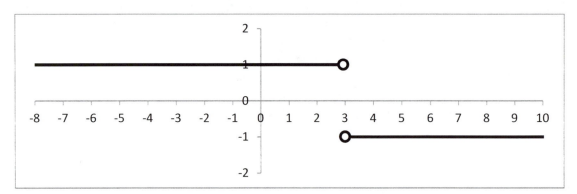

The value of the function approaches –1 as x approaches three from the right, so $\lim_{x \to 3^+} \frac{|x-3|}{3-x} = -1$.

108. C: The slope of the line tangent to the graph of a function f at $x = a$ is $f'(a)$. Since $f(x) = \frac{1}{4}x^2 - 3$, $f'(x) = 2\left(\frac{1}{4}\right)x^{(2-1)} - 0 = \frac{1}{2}x$. So, the slope at $x = 2$ is $f'(2) = \frac{1}{2}(2) = 1$.

109. D: The definition of the derivative of f at 2, or $f'(2)$, is the limit of the difference quotient $\lim_{h \to 0} \frac{f(2+h) - f(2)}{h}$. Rather than find the limit, simply evaluate the derivative of the function at $x = 2$:

$$f(x) = 2x^3 - 3x^2 + 4$$
$$f'(x) = 6x^2 - 6x$$
$$f'(2) = 6(2)^2 - 6(2)$$
$$f'(2) = 12$$

110. D: To find the derivative of $y = e^{3x^2 - 1}$, use the Chain Rule. Let $u = 3x^2 - 1$. Thus, $y = e^u$, and $\frac{dy}{du} = e^u$. Since $\frac{dy}{dx} = \frac{dy}{du} \cdot \frac{du}{dx}$, and since $\frac{du}{dx} = 6x$, $\frac{dy}{dx} = e^{3x^2 - 1} \cdot 6x = 6x\, e^{3x^2 - 1}$.

111. C: To find the derivative of $y = \ln(2x + 1)$, use the Chain Rule. Let $u = 2x + 1$. Thus, $y = \ln u$, and $\frac{dy}{du} = \frac{1}{u}$. Since $\frac{dy}{dx} = \frac{dy}{du} \cdot \frac{du}{dx}$, and since $\frac{du}{dx} = 2$, $\frac{dy}{dx} = \left(\frac{1}{2x+1}\right)(2) = \frac{2}{2x+1}$.

112. A: If $\lim_{x \to a^+} f(x) = \lim_{x \to a^-} f(x)$, then $\lim_{x \to a^+} f(x) = \lim_{x \to a^-} f(x) = \lim_{x \to a} f(x)$. Otherwise, $\lim_{x \to a} f(x)$ does not exist. If $\lim_{x \to a} f(x)$ exists, and if $\lim_{x \to a} f(x) = f(a)$, then the function is continuous at a. Otherwise, f is discontinuous at a.

113. A: To find the second derivative of the function, take the derivative of the first derivative of the function:

$$f(x) = 2x^4 - 4x^3 + 2x^2 - x + 1$$
$$f'(x) = 8x^3 - 12x^2 + 4x - 1$$
$$f''(x) = 24x^2 - 24x + 4.$$

114. A: The critical points of the graph occur when $f'(x) = 0$.

$$f(x) = 4x^3 - x^2 - 4x + 2$$
$$f'(x) = 12x^2 - 2x - 4$$
$$= 2(6x^2 - x - 2)$$
$$= 2(3x - 2)(2x + 1)$$

$$0 = 2(3x - 2)(2x + 1)$$
$$3x - 2 = 0 \quad 2x + 1 = 0$$
$$x = \frac{2}{3} \quad x = -\frac{1}{2}$$

If $f''(x) > 0$ for all x in an interval, the graph of the function is concave upward on that interval, and if $f''(x) < 0$ for all x in an interval, the graph of the function is concave upward on that interval. Find the second derivative of the function and determine the intervals in which $f''(x)$ is less than zero and greater than zero:

$$f''(x) = 24x - 2$$
$$24x - 2 < 0 \quad 24x - 2 > 0$$
$$x < \frac{1}{12} \quad x > \frac{1}{12}$$

The graph of f is concave downward on the interval $\left(-\infty, -\frac{1}{12}\right)$ and concave upward on the interval $\left(-\frac{1}{12}, \infty\right)$. The inflection point of the graph is $\left(\frac{1}{12}, f\left(\frac{1}{12}\right)\right) = \left(\frac{1}{12}, \frac{359}{216}\right)$. The point $\left(\frac{2}{3}, f\left(\frac{2}{3}\right)\right) = \left(\frac{2}{3}, \frac{2}{27}\right)$ is a relative minimum and the point $\left(-\frac{1}{2}, f\left(-\frac{1}{2}\right)\right) = \left(-\frac{1}{2}, 3\frac{1}{4}\right)$ is a relative maximum.

115. D: The velocity v of the ball at any time t is the slope of the line tangent to the graph of h at time t. The slope of a line tangent to the curve $h = -16t^2 + 50t + 3$ is h'.

$$h' = v = -32t + 50$$

When $t = 2$, the velocity of the ball is $-32(2) + 50 = -14$. The velocity is negative because the slope of the tangent line at $t = 2$ is negative; velocity has both magnitude and direction, so a velocity of -14 means that the velocity is 14 ft/s downward.

116. B: The manufacturer wishes to minimize the surface area A of the can while keeping its volume V fixed at 0.5 L = 500 mL = 500 cm^3. The formula for the surface area of a cylinder is $A = 2\pi r h + 2\pi r^2$, and the formula for volume is $V = \pi r^2 h$. To combine the two formulas into one, solve the volume formula for r or h and substitute the resulting expression into the surface area formula for r or h. The volume of the cylinder is 500 cm^3, so $500 = \pi r^2 h \rightarrow h = \frac{500}{\pi r^2}$. Therefore, $A = 2\pi r h + 2\pi r^2 \rightarrow 2\pi r \left(\frac{500}{\pi r^2}\right) + 2\pi r^2 = \frac{1000}{r} + 2\pi r^2$. Find the critical point(s) by setting the first derivative equal to zero and solving for r. Note that r represents the radius of the can and must therefore be a positive number.

$$A = 1000r^{-1} + 2\pi r^2$$
$$A' = -1000r^{-2} + 4\pi r$$
$$0 = -\frac{1000}{r^2} + 4\pi r$$
$$\frac{1000}{r^2} = 4\pi r$$
$$1000 = 4\pi r^3$$
$$\sqrt[3]{\frac{1000}{4\pi}} = r$$

So, when r≈4.3 cm, the minimum surface area is obtained. When the radius of the can is 4.30 cm, its height is $h \approx \frac{500}{\pi(4.30)^2} \approx 8.6$ cm, and the surface area is approximately $\frac{1000}{4.3} + 2\pi(4.3)^2 \approx 348.73$ cm^2. Confirm that the surface area is greater when the radius is slightly smaller or larger than 4.3 cm. For instance, when r=4 cm, the surface area is approximately 350.5 cm^2, and when r=4.5 cm, the surface area is approximately 349.5 cm^2.

117. C: Partitioned into rectangles with length of 1, the left Riemann sum is
20+25+28+30+29+26+22+16+12+10+10+13=241 square units, and the right Riemann sum is
25+28+30+29+26+22+16+12+10+10+13+17=238 square units.

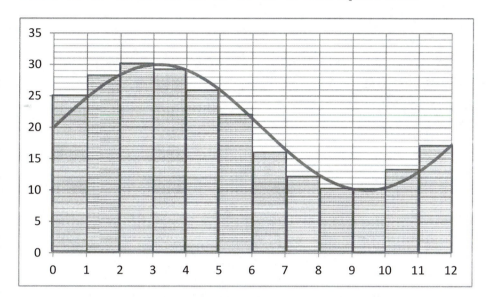

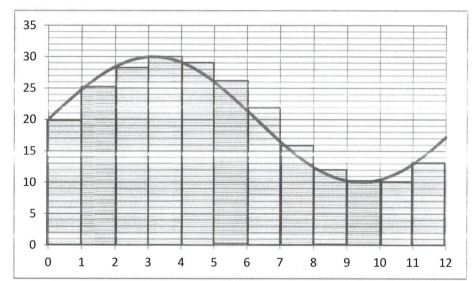

118. B: The area under curve $f(x)$ is $\int_1^2 \frac{1}{x} = [\ln(2)] - [\ln(1)] \approx 0.69$.

119. A: $\int 3x^2 + 2x - 1 = \frac{3}{2+1} x^{2+1} + \frac{2}{1+1} x^{1+1} - x + c = x^3 + x^2 - x + c$.

120. B: To calculate $\int 3x^2 e^{x^3} dx$, let $u = x^3$. Since $du = 3x^2 dx$, $\int 3x^2 e^{x^3} dx = \int e^u du \rightarrow e^u + c \rightarrow e^{x^3} + c$.

121. B: Find the points of intersection of the two graphs:
$$x^2 - 4 = -x + 2$$
$$x^2 + x - 6 = 0$$
$$(x + 3)(x - 2) = 0$$
$$x = -3 \quad x = 2$$

The finite region is bound at the top by the line $y = -x + 2$ and at the bottom by $y = x^2 - 4$, so the area is between the graphs on [-3,2], and the height of the region at point x is defined by $[(-x + 2) - (x^2 - 4)]$. Thus, the area of the region is

$$A = \int_{-3}^{2} [(-x + 2) - (x^2 - 4)]dx$$

$$= \int_{-3}^{2} (-x^2 - x + 6)\, dx$$

$$= \left[-\frac{1}{3}(2)^3 - \frac{1}{2}(2)^2 + 6(2)\right] - \left[-\frac{1}{3}(-3)^3 - \frac{1}{2}(-3)^2 + 6(-3)\right]$$

$$= \left[-\frac{8}{3} - 2 + 12\right] - \left[9 - \frac{9}{2} - 18\right] = \frac{22}{3} - \left(-\frac{27}{2}\right) = \frac{125}{6}$$

122. C: The acceleration a of an object at time t is the derivative of the velocity v of the object at time t, which is the derivative of the position x of the object at time t. So, given the velocity of an object at time t, $x(t)$ can be found by taking the integral of the $v(t)$, and $a(t)$ can be found by taking the derivative of $v(t)$.

$x(t) = \int v(t)dt = \int (12t - t^2)dt = 6t^2 - \frac{1}{3}t^3 + c$. Since the position of the car at time 0 is 0, $v(0) = 0 = 6(0)^2 - \frac{1}{3}(0)^3 + c \to 0 = 0 - 0 + c \to c = 0$. Therefore, $x(t) = 6t^2 - \frac{1}{3}t^3$.

$a(t) = v'(t) = 12 - 2t$.

Find the time at which the acceleration is equal to 0: $0 = 12 - 2t \to t = 6$. Then, find $x(6)$ to find the position of the car when the velocity is 0: $6(6)^2 - \frac{1}{3}(6)^3 = 216 - 72 = 144$.

123. D: To draw a box-and-whisker plot from the data, find the median, quartiles, and upper and lower limits.

```
3 | 6 7 9 9
4 | 2 3 8 8 9          Key
5 | 0 1 1 1 5 7      3|6 = 36
6 | 0 0 1 2 3
```

The median is $\frac{50+51}{2} = 50.5$, the lower quartile is $\frac{22+23}{2} = 22.5$, and the upper quartile is $\frac{57+60}{2} = 58.5$. The box of the box-and-whisker plot goes through the quartiles, and a line through the box represents the median of the data. The whiskers extend from the box to the lower and upper limits, unless there are any outliers in the set. In this case, there are no outliers, so the box-and-whisker plot in choice A correctly represents the data set.

To draw a pie chart, find the percentage of data contained in each of the ranges shown. There are four out of twenty numbers between 30 and 39, inclusive, so the percentage shown in the pie chart for that range of data is $\frac{4}{20} \cdot 100\% = 20\%$; there are five values between 40 to 49, inclusive, so the percentage of data for that sector is $\frac{5}{20} \cdot 100\% = 25\%$; $\frac{6}{20} \cdot 100\% = 30\%$ of the data is within the range of 50-59, and $\frac{5}{20} \cdot 100\% = 25\%$ is within the range of 60-69. The pie chart shows the correct percentage of data in each category.

To draw a cumulative frequency histogram, find the cumulative frequency of the data.

Range	Frequency	Cumulative frequency
30-39	4	4
40-49	5	9
50-59	6	15
60-69	5	20

The histogram shows the correct cumulative frequencies.

Therefore, all of the graphs represent the data set.

124. B: A line graph is often used to show change over time. A Venn diagram shows the relationships among sets. A box and whisker plot shows displays how numeric data are distributed throughout the range. A pie chart shows the relationship of parts to a whole.

125. B: In choice A, the teacher surveys all the members of the population in which he is interested. However, since the response is voluntary, the survey is biased: the participants are self-selected rather than randomly selected. It may be that students who have a strong opinion are more likely to respond than those who are more neutral, and this would give the teacher a skewed perspective of student opinions. In choice B, students are randomly selected, so the sampling technique is not biased. In choice C, the student uses convenience sampling, which is a biased technique. For example, perhaps the student is in an honors class; his sampling method would not be representative of the entire class of eleventh graders, which includes both students who take and who do not take honors classes. Choice D also represents convenience sampling; only the opinions of parents in the PTA are examined, and these parents' opinions may not reflect the opinions of all parents of students at the school.

126. A: Nominal data are data that are collected which have no intrinsic quantity or order. For instance, a survey might ask the respondent to identify his or her gender. While it is possible to compare the relative frequency of each response (for example, "most of the respondents are women"), it is not possible to calculate the mean, which requires data to be numeric, or median, which requires data to be ordered. Interval data are both numeric and ordered, so mean and median can be determined, as can the mode, the interval within which there are the most data. Ordinal data has an inherent order, but there is not a set interval between two points. For example, a survey might ask whether the respondent whether he or she was very dissatisfied, dissatisfied, neutral, satisfied, or very satisfied with the customer service received. Since the data are not numeric, the mean cannot be calculated, but since ordering the data is possible, the median has context.

127. A: The average number of male students in the 11th and 12th grades is 134 males. The number of Hispanic students at the school is 10% of 1219, which is 122 students. The difference in the number of male and female students at the school is $630 - 589 = 41$, and the difference in the number of 9th and 12th grade students at the school is $354 - 255 = 99$.

128. C: 52% of the student population is white. There are 630 female students at the school out of 1219 students, so the percentage of female students is $\frac{630}{1219} \cdot 100\% \approx 52\%$. The percentages rounded to the nearest whole number are the same.

129. D: 131 of 283 eleventh graders are male. Given that an 11th grader is chosen to attend the conference, the probability that a male is chosen is $\frac{\text{number of males}}{\text{number of 11th graders}} = \frac{131}{283} \approx 0.46$. Note that this is **NOT** the same question as one which asks for the probability of selecting at random from the school a male student who is in eleventh grade, which has a probability of $\frac{131}{1219} \approx 0.11$.

130. A: The range is the spread of the data. It can be calculated for each class by subtracting the lowest test score from the highest, or it can be determined visually from the graph. The difference between the highest and lowest test scores in class A is 98-23=75 points. The range for each of the other classes is much smaller.

131. D: 75% of the data in a set is above the first quartile. Since the first quartile for this set is 73, there is a 75% chance that a student chosen at random from class 2 scored above a 73.

132. C: The line through the center of the box represents the median. The median test score for classes 1 and 2 is 82.

Note that for class 1, the median is a better representation of the data than the mean. There are two outliers (points which lie outside of two standard deviations from the mean) which bring down the average test score. In cases such as this, the mean is not the best measure of central tendency.

133. D:

Time on market	Frequency for Zip Code 1	Frequency for Zip Code 2	Time·Frequency for Zip Code 1	Time·Frequency for Zip Code 1
1	9	6	9	6
2	10	4	20	8
3	12	3	36	9
4	8	4	32	16
5	6	3	30	15
6	5	5	30	30
7	8	2	56	14
8	8	1	64	8
9	6	3	54	27
10	3	5	30	50
11	5	7	55	77
12	4	6	48	72
13	2	6	26	78
14	3	5	42	70
15	1	3	15	45
16	2	2	32	32
17	2	3	34	51
18	1	5	18	90
19	0	6	0	114
20	2	4	40	80
21	1	5	21	105
22	1	4	22	88
23	0	3	0	69
24	1	5	24	120
SUM	100	100	738	1274

Since there are 100 homes' market times represented in each set, the median time a home spends on the market is between the 50th and 51st data point in each set. The 50th and 51st data points for Zip Code 1 are six months and seven months, respectively, so the median time a house in Zip Code 1 spends on the market is between six and seven months (6.5 months), which by the realtor's definition of market time is a seven month market time. The 50th and 51st data points for Zip Code 2 are both thirteen months, so the median time a house in Zip Code 2 spends on the market is thirteen months.

To find the mean market time for 100 houses, find the sum of the market times and divide by 100. If the frequency of a one month market time is 9, the number 1 is added nine times (1·9), if frequency of a two month market time is 10, the number 2 is added ten times (2·10), and so on. So, to find the average market time, divide by 100 the sum of the products of each market time and its corresponding frequency. For Zip Code 1, the mean market time is 7.38 months, which by the realtor's definition of market time is an eight month market time. For Zip Code 2, the mean market time is 12.74, which by the realtor's definition of market time is a thirteen month market time.

The mode market time is the market time for which the frequency is the highest. For Zip Code 1, the mode market time is three months, and for Zip Code 2, the mode market time is eleven months.

The statement given in choice D is true. The median time a house spends on the market in Zip Code 1 is less than the mean time a house spends on the market in Zip Code 1.

134. C: The probability of an event is the number of possible occurrences of that event divided by the number of all possible outcomes. A camper who is at least eight years old can be eight, nine, or ten years old, so the probability of randomly selecting a camper at least eight years old is

$$\frac{\text{number of eight-, nine-, and ten-year old campers}}{\text{total number of campers}} = \frac{14+12+10}{12+15+14+12+10} = \frac{36}{63} = \frac{4}{7}.$$

135. B:

	Department 1	Department 2	Department 3	Total
Women	12	28	16	56
Men	18	14	15	47
Total	30	42	31	103

There are three ways in which two women from the same department can be selected: two women can be selected from the first department, or two women can be selected from the second department, or two women can be selected from the third department. The probability that two women are selected from Department 1 is $\frac{12}{103} \cdot \frac{11}{102} = \frac{132}{10506}$, the probability that two women are selected from Department 2 is $\frac{28}{103} \cdot \frac{27}{102} = \frac{756}{10506}$, and the probability that two women are selected from Department 3 is $\frac{16}{103} \cdot \frac{15}{102} = \frac{240}{10506}$. Since any of these is a discrete possible outcome, the probability that two women will be selected from the same department is the sum of these outcomes: $\frac{132}{10506} + \frac{756}{10506} + \frac{240}{10506} \approx 0.107$, or 10.7%.

136. B: The number of students who like broccoli is equal to the number of students who like all three vegetables plus the number of students who like broccoli and carrots but not cauliflower plus the number of students who like broccoli and cauliflower but not carrots plus the number of students who like broccoli but no other vegetable: $3 + 15 + 4 + 10 = 32$. These students plus the numbers of students who like just cauliflower, just carrots, cauliflower and carrots, or none of the vegetables represents the entire set of students sampled: $32 + 2 + 27 + 6 + 23 = 90$. So, the probability that a randomly chosen student likes broccoli is $\frac{32}{90} \approx 0.356$.

The number of students who like carrots and at least one other vegetable is $15 + 6 + 3 = 24$. The number of students who like carrots is $24 + 27 = 51$. So, the probability that a student who likes carrots will also like at least one other vegetable is $\frac{24}{51} \approx 0.471$. The number of students who like cauliflower and broccoli is $4 + 3 = 7$. The number of students who like all three vegetables is 3. So, the probability that a student who likes cauliflower and broccoli will also like carrots is $\frac{3}{7} \approx 0.429$.

the theoretical probability, one would expect 5,000 members of a population of 100,000 to be homozygous for a or b.

141. D: A score of 85 is one standard deviation below the mean. Since approximately 68% of the data is within one standard deviation of the mean, about 32% (100%-68%) of the data is outside of one standard deviation within the mean. Normally distributed data is symmetric about the mean, which means that about 16% of the data lies below one standard deviation below the mean and about 16% of data lies above one standard deviation above the mean. Therefore, approximately 16% of individuals have IQs less than 85, while approximately 84% of the population has an IQ of at least 85. Since 84% of 300 is 252, about 252 people from the selected group have IQs of at least 85.

142. C: There are nine ways to assign the first digit since it can be any of the numbers 1-9. There are nine ways to assign the second digit since it can be any digit 0-9 EXCEPT for the digit assigned in place 1. There are eight ways to assign the third number since there are ten digits, two of which have already been assigned. There are seven ways to assign the fourth number, six ways to assign the fifth, five ways to assign the sixth, and four ways to assign the seventh. So, the number of combinations is $9 \cdot 9 \cdot 8 \cdot 7 \cdot 6 \cdot 5 \cdot 4 = 544,320$.

Another way to approach the problem is to notice that the arrangement of nine digits in the last six places is a sequence without reputation, or a permutation. (Note: this may be called a partial permutation since all of the elements of the set need not be used.) The number of possible sequences of a fixed length r of elements taken from a given set of size n is permutation $_nP_r = \dfrac{n!}{(n-r)!}$. So, the number of ways to arrange the last six digits is $_9P_6 = \dfrac{9!}{(9-6)!} = \dfrac{9!}{3!} = 60,480$. Multiply this number by nine since there are nine possibilities for the first digit of the phone number. $9 \cdot _9P_6 = 544,320$.

143. B: If each of the four groups in the class of twenty will contain three boys and two girls, there must be twelve boys and eight girls in the class. The number of ways the teacher can select three boys from a group of twelve boys is $_{12}C_3 = \dfrac{12!}{3!(12-3)!} = \dfrac{12!}{3!9!} = \dfrac{12 \cdot 11 \cdot 10 \cdot 9!}{3!9!} = \dfrac{12 \cdot 11 \cdot 10}{3 \cdot 2 \cdot 1} = 220$. The number of ways she can select two girls from a group of eight girls is $_8C_2 = \dfrac{8!}{2!(8-2)!} = \dfrac{8!}{2!6!} = \dfrac{8 \cdot 7 \cdot 6!}{2!6!} = \dfrac{8 \cdot 7}{2 \cdot 1} = 28$. Since each combination of boys can be paired with each combination of girls, the number of group combinations is $220 \cdot 28 = 6,160$.

144. B: One way to approach this problem is to first consider the number of arrangements of the five members of the family if Tasha (T) and Mac (M) must sit together. Treat them as a unit seated in a fixed location at the table; then arrange the other three family members (A, B, and C):

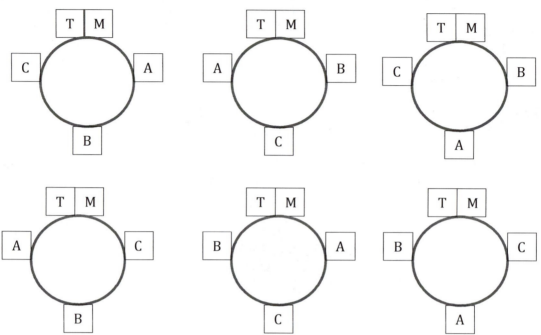

There are six ways to arrange four units around a circle as shown. (Any other arrangement would be a rotation in which the elements in the same order and would therefore not be a unique arrangement.) Note that there are $(n - 1)!$ ways to arrange n units around a circle for $n > 1$.

Of course, Mac and Tasha are not actually a single unit. They would still be sitting beside each other if they were to trade seats, so there are twelve arrangements in which the two are seated next to one another. In all other arrangements of the five family members, they are separated. Therefore, to find the number of arrangements in which Tasha and Mac are not sitting together, subtract twelve from the possible arrangement of five units around a circle: $(5 - 1)! - 12 = 12$.

145. A: The recursive definition of the sequence gives the first term of the series, $a_1 = -1$. The definition also defines each term in the series as the sum of the previous term and 2. Therefore, the second term in the series is $-1 + 2 = 1$, the third term in the series is $1 + 2 = 3$, and so on.

n	a_n
1	-1
2	1
3	3

The relationship between n and a_n is linear, so the equation of the sequence can be found in the same way as the equation of a line. The value of a_n increases by two each time the value of n increases by 1.

n	$2n$	a_n
1	2	-1
2	4	1
3	6	3

Since the difference in $2n$ and a_n is 3, $a_n = 2n - 3$.

n	$2n - 3$	a_n
1	2-3	-1
2	4-3	1
3	6-3	3

146. B: The series is an infinite geometric series, the sum of which can be found by using the formula $\sum_{n=0}^{\infty} ar^n = \frac{a}{1-r}, |r| < 1$, where a is the first term in the series and r is the ratio between successive terms. In the series 200+100+50+25+ ..., $a = 200$ and $r = \frac{1}{2}$. So, the sum of the series is $\frac{200}{1-\frac{1}{2}} = \frac{200}{\frac{1}{2}} = 400$.

147. A: The sum of two vectors is equal to the sum of their components. Using component-wise addition, $v + w = (4 + (-3), 3 + 4) = (1,7)$. To multiply a vector by a scalar, multiply each component by that scalar. Using component-wise scalar multiplication, $2(1,7) = (2 \cdot 1, 2 \cdot 7) = (2,14)$.

148. A: First, subtract the two column matrices in parentheses by subtracting corresponding terms.
$$[2 \quad 0 \quad -5]\left(\begin{bmatrix} 4-3 \\ 2-5 \\ -1-(-5) \end{bmatrix}\right) = [2 \quad 0 \quad -5]\begin{bmatrix} 1 \\ -3 \\ 4 \end{bmatrix}$$
Then, multiply the matrices. The product of a 1×3 matrix and a 3×1 matrix is a 1×1 matrix.
$$[2 \quad 0 \quad -5]\begin{bmatrix} 1 \\ -3 \\ 4 \end{bmatrix} = [(2)(1) + (0)(-3) + (-5)(4)] = [-18]$$

Note that matrix multiplication is NOT commutative. The product of the 3x1 matrix $\begin{bmatrix} 1 \\ -3 \\ 4 \end{bmatrix}$ and the 1x3

matrix $[2 \quad 0 \quad -5]$ is the 3x3 matrix $\begin{bmatrix} 2 & 0 & -5 \\ -6 & 0 & 15 \\ 8 & 0 & -20 \end{bmatrix}$.

149. B: The table below shows the intersections of each set with each of the other sets.

Set	{2,4,6,8,10,12,...}	{1,2,3,4,6,12}	{1,2,4,9}
{2,4,6,8,10,12,... }	{2,4,6,8,10,12,...}	{2,4,6,12}	{2,4}
{1,2,3,4,6,12}	{2,4,6,12}	{1,2,3,4,6,12}	{1,2,4}
{1,2,4,9}	{2,4}	{1,2,4}	{1,2,4,9}

Notice that {2,4} is a subset of {2,4,6,12} and {1,2,4}. So, the intersection of {1,2,4,9} and the even integers is a subset of the intersection of the even integers and the factors of twelve, and the intersection of the set of even integers and {1,2,4,9} is a subset of the intersection of {1,2,4,9} and the factors of twelve. So, while it is not possible to determine which set is A and which is B, set C must be the set of factors of twelve: {1,2,3,4,6,12}.

150. D: Use a Venn diagram to help organize the given information. Start by filling in the space where the three circles intersect: Jenny tutored three students in all three areas. Use that information to fill in the spaces where two circles intersect: for example, she tutored four students in chemistry and for the ACT, and three of those were students she tutored in all three areas, so one student was tutored in chemistry and for the ACT but not for math. Once the diagram is completed, add the number of students who were tutored in all areas to the number of students tutored in only two of the three areas to the number of students tutored in only one area. The total number of students tutored was 3+2+2+1+3+2+1=14.

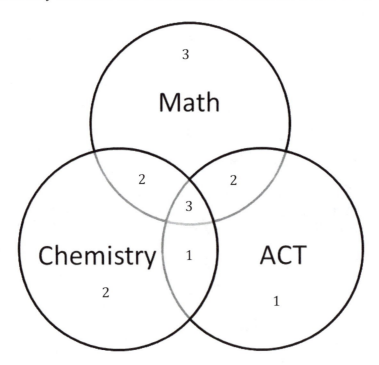

Secret Key #1 - Time is Your Greatest Enemy

Pace Yourself

Wear a watch. At the beginning of the test, check the time (or start a chronometer on your watch to count the minutes), and check the time after every few questions to make sure you are "on schedule."

If you are forced to speed up, do it efficiently. Usually one or more answer choices can be eliminated without too much difficulty. Above all, don't panic. Don't speed up and just begin guessing at random choices. By pacing yourself, and continually monitoring your progress against your watch, you will always know exactly how far ahead or behind you are with your available time. If you find that you are one minute behind on the test, don't skip one question without spending any time on it, just to catch back up. Take 15 fewer seconds on the next four questions, and after four questions you'll have caught back up. Once you catch back up, you can continue working each problem at your normal pace.

Furthermore, don't dwell on the problems that you were rushed on. If a problem was taking up too much time and you made a hurried guess, it must be difficult. The difficult questions are the ones you are most likely to miss anyway, so it isn't a big loss. It is better to end with more time than you need than to run out of time.

Lastly, sometimes it is beneficial to slow down if you are constantly getting ahead of time. You are always more likely to catch a careless mistake by working more slowly than quickly, and among very high-scoring test takers (those who are likely to have lots of time left over), careless errors affect the score more than mastery of material.

Secret Key #2 - Guessing is not Guesswork

You probably know that guessing is a good idea. Unlike other standardized tests, there is no penalty for getting a wrong answer. Even if you have no idea about a question, you still have a 20-25% chance of getting it right.

Most test takers do not understand the impact that proper guessing can have on their score. Unless you score extremely high, guessing will significantly contribute to your final score.

Monkeys Take the Test

What most test takers don't realize is that to insure that 20-25% chance, you have to guess randomly. If you put 20 monkeys in a room to take this test, assuming they answered once per question and behaved themselves, on average they would get 20-25% of the questions correct. Put 20 test takers in the room, and the average will be much lower among guessed questions. Why?

1. The test writers intentionally write deceptive answer choices that "look" right. A test taker has no idea about a question, so he picks the "best looking" answer, which is often wrong. The monkey has no idea what looks good and what doesn't, so it will consistently be right about 20-25% of the time.

2. Test takers will eliminate answer choices from the guessing pool based on a hunch or intuition. Simple but correct answers often get excluded, leaving a 0% chance of being correct. The monkey has no clue, and often gets lucky with the best choice.

This is why the process of elimination endorsed by most test courses is flawed and detrimental to your performance. Test takers don't guess; they make an ignorant stab in the dark that is usually worse than random.

$5 Challenge

Let me introduce one of the most valuable ideas of this course—the $5 challenge:
- *You only mark your "best guess" if you are willing to bet $5 on it.*
- *You only eliminate choices from guessing if you are willing to bet $5 on it.*

Why $5? Five dollars is an amount of money that is small yet not insignificant, and can really add up fast (20 questions could cost you $100). Likewise, each answer choice on one question of the test will have a small impact on your overall score, but it can really add up to a lot of points in the end.

The process of elimination IS valuable. The following shows your chance of guessing it right:

If you eliminate wrong answer choices until only this many remain:	Chance of getting it correct:
1	100%
2	50%
3	33%

However, if you accidentally eliminate the right answer or go on a hunch for an incorrect answer, your chances drop dramatically—to 0%. By guessing among all the answer choices, you are GUARANTEED to have a shot at the right answer.

That's why the $5 test is so valuable. If you give up the advantage and safety of a pure guess, it had better be worth the risk.

What we still haven't covered is how to be sure that whatever guess you make is truly random. Here's the easiest way:
- *Always pick the first answer choice among those remaining.*

Such a technique means that you have decided, **before you see a single test question**, exactly how you are going to guess, and since the order of choices tells you nothing about which one is correct, this guessing technique is perfectly random.

This section is not meant to scare you away from making educated guesses or eliminating choices; you just need to define when a choice is worth eliminating. The $5 test, along with a pre-defined random guessing strategy, is the best way to make sure you reap all of the benefits of guessing.

Secret Key #3 - Practice Smarter, Not Harder

Many test takers delay the test preparation process because they dread the awful amounts of practice time they think necessary to succeed on the test. We have refined an effective method that will take you only a fraction of the time.

There are a number of "obstacles" in the path to success. Among these are answering questions, finishing in time, and mastering test-taking strategies. All must be executed on the day of the test at peak performance, or your score will suffer. The test is a mental marathon that has a large impact on your future.

Just like a marathon runner, it is important to work your way up to the full challenge. So first you just worry about questions, and then time, and finally strategy:

Success Strategy

1. Find a good source for practice tests.
2. If you are willing to make a larger time investment, consider using more than one study guide. Often the different approaches of multiple authors will help you "get" difficult concepts.
3. Take a practice test with no time constraints, with all study helps, "open book." Take your time with questions and focus on applying strategies.
4. Take a practice test with time constraints, with all guides, "open book."
5. Take a final practice test without open material and with time limits.

If you have time to take more practice tests, just repeat step 5. By gradually exposing yourself to the full rigors of the test environment, you will condition your mind to the stress of test day and maximize your success.

Secret Key #4 - Prepare, Don't Procrastinate

Let me state an obvious fact: if you take the test three times, you will probably get three different scores. This is due to the way you feel on test day, the level of preparedness you have, and the version of the test you see. Despite the test writers' claims to the contrary, some versions of the test WILL be easier for you than others.

Since your future depends so much on your score, you should maximize your chances of success. In order to maximize the likelihood of success, you've got to prepare in advance. This means taking practice tests and spending time learning the information and test taking strategies you will need to succeed.

Never go take the actual test as a "practice" test, expecting that you can just take it again if you need to. Take all the practice tests you can on your own, but when you go to take the official test, be prepared, be focused, and do your best the first time!

Secret Key #5 - Test Yourself

Everyone knows that time is money. There is no need to spend too much of your time or too little of your time preparing for the test. You should only spend as much of your precious time preparing as is necessary for you to get the score you need.

Once you have taken a practice test under real conditions of time constraints, then you will know if you are ready for the test or not.

If you have scored extremely high the first time that you take the practice test, then there is not much point in spending countless hours studying. You are already there.

Benchmark your abilities by retaking practice tests and seeing how much you have improved. Once you consistently score high enough to guarantee success, then you are ready.

If you have scored well below where you need, then knuckle down and begin studying in earnest. Check your improvement regularly through the use of practice tests under real conditions. Above all, don't worry, panic, or give up. The key is perseverance!

Then, when you go to take the test, remain confident and remember how well you did on the practice tests. If you can score high enough on a practice test, then you can do the same on the real thing.

General Strategies

The most important thing you can do is to ignore your fears and jump into the test immediately. Do not be overwhelmed by any strange-sounding terms. You have to jump into the test like jumping into a pool—all at once is the easiest way.

Make Predictions

As you read and understand the question, try to guess what the answer will be. Remember that several of the answer choices are wrong, and once you begin reading them, your mind will immediately become cluttered with answer choices designed to throw you off. Your mind is typically the most focused immediately after you have read the question and digested its contents. If you can, try to predict what the correct answer will be. You may be surprised at what you can predict.

Quickly scan the choices and see if your prediction is in the listed answer choices. If it is, then you can be quite confident that you have the right answer. It still won't hurt to check the other answer choices, but most of the time, you've got it!

Answer the Question

It may seem obvious to only pick answer choices that answer the question, but the test writers can create some excellent answer choices that are wrong. Don't pick an answer just because it sounds right, or you believe it to be true. It MUST answer the question. Once you've made your selection, always go back and check it against the question and make sure that you didn't misread the question and that the answer choice does answer the question posed.

Benchmark

After you read the first answer choice, decide if you think it sounds correct or not. If it doesn't, move on to the next answer choice. If it does, mentally mark that answer choice. This doesn't mean that you've definitely selected it as your answer choice, it just means that it's the best you've seen thus far. Go ahead and read the next choice. If the next choice is worse than the one you've already selected, keep going to the next answer choice. If the next choice is better than the choice you've already selected, mentally mark the new answer choice as your best guess.

The first answer choice that you select becomes your standard. Every other answer choice must be benchmarked against that standard. That choice is correct until proven otherwise by another answer choice beating it out. Once you've decided that no other answer choice seems as good, do one final check to ensure that your answer choice answers the question posed.

Valid Information

Don't discount any of the information provided in the question. Every piece of information may be necessary to determine the correct answer. None of the information in the question is there to throw you off (while the answer choices will certainly have information to throw you off). If two seemingly unrelated topics are discussed, don't ignore either. You can be confident there is a relationship, or it wouldn't be included in the question, and you are probably going to have to determine what is that relationship to find the answer.

Avoid "Fact Traps"

Don't get distracted by a choice that is factually true. Your search is for the answer that answers the question. Stay focused and don't fall for an answer that is true but irrelevant. Always go back to the question and make sure you're choosing an answer that actually answers the question and is not just a true statement. An answer can be factually correct, but it MUST answer the question asked. Additionally, two answers can both be seemingly correct, so be sure to read all of the answer choices, and make sure that you get the one that BEST answers the question.

Milk the Question

Some of the questions may throw you completely off. They might deal with a subject you have not been exposed to, or one that you haven't reviewed in years. While your lack of knowledge about the subject will be a hindrance, the question itself can give you many clues that will help you find the correct answer. Read the question carefully and look for clues. Watch particularly for adjectives and nouns describing difficult terms or words that you don't recognize. Regardless of whether you completely understand a word or not, replacing it with a synonym, either provided or one you more familiar with, may help you to understand what the questions are asking. Rather than wracking your mind about specific detailed information concerning a difficult term or word, try to use mental substitutes that are easier to understand.

The Trap of Familiarity

Don't just choose a word because you recognize it. On difficult questions, you may not recognize a number of words in the answer choices. The test writers don't put "make-believe" words on the test, so don't think that just because you only recognize all the words in one answer choice that that answer choice must be correct. If you only recognize words in one answer choice, then focus on that one. Is it correct? Try your best to determine if it is correct. If it is, that's great. If not, eliminate it. Each word and answer choice you eliminate increases your chances of getting the question correct, even if you then have to guess among the unfamiliar choices.

Eliminate Answers

Eliminate choices as soon as you realize they are wrong. But be careful! Make sure you consider all of the possible answer choices. Just because one appears right, doesn't mean that the next one won't be even better! The test writers will usually put more than one good answer choice for every question, so read all of them. Don't worry if you are stuck between two that seem right. By getting down to just two remaining possible choices, your odds are now 50/50. Rather than wasting too much time, play the odds. You are guessing, but guessing wisely because you've been able to knock out some of the answer choices that you know are wrong. If you are eliminating choices and realize that the last answer choice you are left with is also obviously wrong, don't panic. Start over and consider each choice again. There may easily be something that you missed the first time and will realize on the second pass.

Tough Questions

If you are stumped on a problem or it appears too hard or too difficult, don't waste time. Move on! Remember though, if you can quickly check for obviously incorrect answer choices, your chances of guessing correctly are greatly improved. Before you completely give up, at least try to knock out a couple of possible answers. Eliminate what you can and then guess at the remaining answer choices before moving on.

Brainstorm

If you get stuck on a difficult question, spend a few seconds quickly brainstorming. Run through the complete list of possible answer choices. Look at each choice and ask yourself, "Could this answer the question satisfactorily?" Go through each answer choice and consider it independently of the others. By systematically going through all possibilities, you may find something that you would otherwise overlook. Remember though that when you get stuck, it's important to try to keep moving.

Read Carefully

Understand the problem. Read the question and answer choices carefully. Don't miss the question because you misread the terms. You have plenty of time to read each question thoroughly and make sure you understand what is being asked. Yet a happy medium must be attained, so don't waste too much time. You must read carefully, but efficiently.

Face Value

When in doubt, use common sense. Always accept the situation in the problem at face value. Don't read too much into it. These problems will not require you to make huge leaps of logic. The test writers aren't trying to throw you off with a cheap trick. If you have to go beyond creativity and make a leap of logic in order to have an answer choice answer the question, then you should look at the other answer choices. Don't overcomplicate the problem by creating theoretical relationships or explanations that will warp time or space. These are normal problems rooted in reality. It's just that the applicable relationship or explanation may not be readily apparent and you have to figure things out. Use your common sense to interpret anything that isn't clear.

Prefixes

If you're having trouble with a word in the question or answer choices, try dissecting it. Take advantage of every clue that the word might include. Prefixes and suffixes can be a huge help. Usually they allow you to determine a basic meaning. Pre- means before, post- means after, pro - is positive, de- is negative. From these prefixes and suffixes, you can get an idea of the general meaning of the word and try to put it into context. Beware though of any traps. Just because con- is the opposite of pro-, doesn't necessarily mean congress is the opposite of progress!

Hedge Phrases

Watch out for critical hedge phrases, led off with words such as "likely," "may," "can," "sometimes," "often," "almost," "mostly," "usually," "generally," "rarely," and "sometimes." Question writers insert these hedge phrases to cover every possibility. Often an answer choice will be wrong simply because it leaves no room for exception. Unless the situation calls for them, avoid answer choices that have definitive words like "exactly," and "always."

Switchback Words

Stay alert for "switchbacks." These are the words and phrases frequently used to alert you to shifts in thought. The most common switchback word is "but." Others include "although," "however," "nevertheless," "on the other hand," "even though," "while," "in spite of," "despite," and "regardless of."

New Information

Correct answer choices will rarely have completely new information included. Answer choices typically are straightforward reflections of the material asked about and will directly relate to the question. If a new piece of information is included in an answer choice that doesn't even seem to relate to the topic being asked about, then that answer choice is likely incorrect. All of the information needed to answer the question is usually provided for you in the question. You should not have to make guesses that are unsupported or choose answer choices that require unknown information that cannot be reasoned from what is given.

Time Management

On technical questions, don't get lost on the technical terms. Don't spend too much time on any one question. If you don't know what a term means, then odds are you aren't going to get much further since you don't have a dictionary. You should be able to immediately recognize whether or not you know a term. If you don't, work with the other clues that you have—the other answer choices and terms provided—but don't waste too much time trying to figure out a difficult term that you don't know.

Contextual Clues

Look for contextual clues. An answer can be right but not the correct answer. The contextual clues will help you find the answer that is most right and is correct. Understand the context in which a phrase or statement is made. This will help you make important distinctions.

Don't Panic

Panicking will not answer any questions for you; therefore, it isn't helpful. When you first see the question, if your mind goes blank, take a deep breath. Force yourself to mechanically go through the steps of solving the problem using the strategies you've learned.

Pace Yourself

Don't get clock fever. It's easy to be overwhelmed when you're looking at a page full of questions, your mind is full of random thoughts and feeling confused, and the clock is ticking down faster than you would like. Calm down and maintain the pace that you have set for yourself. As long as you are on track by monitoring your pace, you are guaranteed to have enough time for yourself. When you get to the last few minutes of the test, it may seem like you won't have enough time left, but if you only have as many questions as you should have left at that point, then you're right on track!

Answer Selection

The best way to pick an answer choice is to eliminate all of those that are wrong, until only one is left and confirm that is the correct answer. Sometimes though, an answer choice may immediately look right. Be careful! Take a second to make sure that the other choices are not equally obvious. Don't make a hasty mistake. There are only two times that you should stop before checking other answers. First is when you are positive that the answer choice you have selected is correct. Second is when time is almost out and you have to make a quick guess!

Check Your Work

Since you will probably not know every term listed and the answer to every question, it is important that you get credit for the ones that you do know. Don't miss any questions through careless mistakes. If at all possible, try to take a second to look back over your answer selection and make sure you've selected the correct answer choice and haven't made a costly careless mistake (such as marking an answer choice that you didn't mean to mark). The time it takes for this quick double check should more than pay for itself in caught mistakes.

Beware of Directly Quoted Answers

Sometimes an answer choice will repeat word for word a portion of the question or reference section. However, beware of such exact duplication. It may be a trap! More than likely, the correct choice will paraphrase or summarize a point, rather than being exactly the same wording.

Slang

Scientific sounding answers are better than slang ones. An answer choice that begins "To compare the outcomes…" is much more likely to be correct than one that begins "Because some people insisted…"

Extreme Statements

Avoid wild answers that throw out highly controversial ideas that are proclaimed as established fact. An answer choice that states the "process should used in certain situations, if…" is much more likely to be correct than one that states the "process should be discontinued completely." The first is a calm rational statement and doesn't even make a definitive, uncompromising stance, using a hedge word "if" to provide wiggle room, whereas the second choice is a radical idea and far more extreme.

Answer Choice Families

When you have two or more answer choices that are direct opposites or parallels, one of them is usually the correct answer. For instance, if one answer choice states "x increases" and another answer choice states "x decreases" or "y increases," then those two or three answer choices are very similar in construction and fall into the same family of answer choices. A family of answer choices consists of two or three answer choices, very similar in construction, but often with directly opposite meanings. Usually the correct answer choice will be in that family of answer choices. The "odd man out" or answer choice that doesn't seem to fit the parallel construction of the other answer choices is more likely to be incorrect.

Special Report: How to Overcome Test Anxiety

The very nature of tests caters to some level of anxiety, nervousness, or tension, just as we feel for any important event that occurs in our lives. A little bit of anxiety or nervousness can be a good thing. It helps us with motivation, and makes achievement just that much sweeter. However, too much anxiety can be a problem, especially if it hinders our ability to function and perform.

"Test anxiety," is the term that refers to the emotional reactions that some test-takers experience when faced with a test or exam. Having a fear of testing and exams is based upon a rational fear, since the test-taker's performance can shape the course of an academic career. Nevertheless, experiencing excessive fear of examinations will only interfere with the test-taker's ability to perform and chance to be successful.

There are a large variety of causes that can contribute to the development and sensation of test anxiety. These include, but are not limited to, lack of preparation and worrying about issues surrounding the test.

Lack of Preparation

Lack of preparation can be identified by the following behaviors or situations:
- Not scheduling enough time to study, and therefore cramming the night before the test or exam
- Managing time poorly, to create the sensation that there is not enough time to do everything
- Failing to organize the text information in advance, so that the study material consists of the entire text and not simply the pertinent information
- Poor overall studying habits

Worrying, on the other hand, can be related to both the test taker, or many other factors around him/her that will be affected by the results of the test. These include worrying about:
- Previous performances on similar exams, or exams in general
- How friends and other students are achieving
- The negative consequences that will result from a poor grade or failure

There are three primary elements to test anxiety. Physical components, which involve the same typical bodily reactions as those to acute anxiety (to be discussed below). Emotional factors have to do with fear or panic. Mental or cognitive issues concerning attention spans and memory abilities.

Physical Signals

There are many different symptoms of test anxiety, and these are not limited to mental and emotional strain. Frequently there are a range of physical signals that will let a test taker know that he/she is suffering from test anxiety. These bodily changes can include the following:

- Perspiring
- Sweaty palms
- Wet, trembling hands
- Nausea
- Dry mouth
- A knot in the stomach
- Headache
- Faintness
- Muscle tension
- Aching shoulders, back and neck
- Rapid heart beat
- Feeling too hot/cold

To recognize the sensation of test anxiety, a test-taker should monitor him/herself for the following sensations:

- The physical distress symptoms as listed above
- Emotional sensitivity, expressing emotional feelings such as the need to cry or laugh too much, or a sensation of anger or helplessness
- A decreased ability to think, causing the test-taker to blank out or have racing thoughts that are hard to organize or control.

Though most students will feel some level of anxiety when faced with a test or exam, the majority can cope with that anxiety and maintain it at a manageable level. However, those who cannot are faced with a very real and very serious condition, which can and should be controlled for the immeasurable benefit of this sufferer.

Naturally, these sensations lead to negative results for the testing experience. The most common effects of test anxiety have to do with nervousness and mental blocking.

Nervousness

Nervousness can appear in several different levels:

- The test-taker's difficulty, or even inability to read and understand the questions on the test
- The difficulty or inability to organize thoughts to a coherent form
- The difficulty or inability to recall key words and concepts relating to the testing questions (especially essays)
- The receipt of poor grades on a test, though the test material was well known by the test taker

Conversely, a person may also experience mental blocking, which involves:

- Blanking out on test questions
- Only remembering the correct answers to the questions when the test has already finished.

Fortunately for test anxiety sufferers, beating these feelings, to a large degree, has to do with proper preparation. When a test taker has a feeling of preparedness, then anxiety will be dramatically lessened.

The first step to resolving anxiety issues is to distinguish which of the two types of anxiety are being suffered. If the anxiety is a direct result of a lack of preparation, this should be considered a normal reaction, and the anxiety level (as opposed to the test results) shouldn't be anything to worry about. However, if, when adequately prepared, the test-taker still panics, blanks out, or seems to overreact, this is not a fully rational reaction. While this can be considered normal too, there are many ways to combat and overcome these effects.

Remember that anxiety cannot be entirely eliminated, however, there are ways to minimize it, to make the anxiety easier to manage. Preparation is one of the best ways to minimize test anxiety. Therefore the following techniques are wise in order to best fight off any anxiety that may want to build.

To begin with, try to avoid cramming before a test, whenever it is possible. By trying to memorize an entire term's worth of information in one day, you'll be shocking your system, and not giving yourself a very good chance to absorb the information. This is an easy path to anxiety, so for those who suffer from test anxiety, cramming should not even be considered an option.

Instead of cramming, work throughout the semester to combine all of the material which is presented throughout the semester, and work on it gradually as the course goes by, making sure to master the main concepts first, leaving minor details for a week or so before the test.

To study for the upcoming exam, be sure to pose questions that may be on the examination, to gauge the ability to answer them by integrating the ideas from your texts, notes and lectures, as well as any supplementary readings.

If it is truly impossible to cover all of the information that was covered in that particular term, concentrate on the most important portions, that can be covered very well. Learn these concepts as best as possible, so that when the test comes, a goal can be made to use these concepts as presentations of your knowledge.

In addition to study habits, changes in attitude are critical to beating a struggle with test anxiety. In fact, an improvement of the perspective over the entire test-taking experience can actually help a test taker to enjoy studying and therefore improve the overall experience. Be certain not to overemphasize the significance of the grade - know that the result of the test is neither a reflection of self worth, nor is it a measure of intelligence; one grade will not predict a person's future success.

To improve an overall testing outlook, the following steps should be tried:
- Keeping in mind that the most reasonable expectation for taking a test is to expect to try to demonstrate as much of what you know as you possibly can.
- Reminding ourselves that a test is only one test; this is not the only one, and there will be others.
- The thought of thinking of oneself in an irrational, all-or-nothing term should be avoided at all costs.
- A reward should be designated for after the test, so there's something to look forward to. Whether it be going to a movie, going out to eat, or simply visiting friends, schedule it in advance, and do it no matter what result is expected on the exam.

Test-takers should also keep in mind that the basics are some of the most important things, even beyond anti-anxiety techniques and studying. Never neglect the basic social, emotional and biological needs, in order to try to absorb information. In order to best achieve, these three factors must be held as just as important as the studying itself.

Study Steps

Remember the following important steps for studying:
- Maintain healthy nutrition and exercise habits. Continue both your recreational activities and social pass times. These both contribute to your physical and emotional well being.
- Be certain to get a good amount of sleep, especially the night before the test, because when you're overtired you are not able to perform to the best of your best ability.
- Keep the studying pace to a moderate level by taking breaks when they are needed, and varying the work whenever possible, to keep the mind fresh instead of getting bored.
- When enough studying has been done that all the material that can be learned has been learned, and the test taker is prepared for the test, stop studying and do something relaxing such as listening to music, watching a movie, or taking a warm bubble bath.

There are also many other techniques to minimize the uneasiness or apprehension that is experienced along with test anxiety before, during, or even after the examination. In fact, there are a great deal of things that can be done to stop anxiety from interfering with lifestyle and performance. Again, remember that anxiety will not be eliminated entirely, and it shouldn't be. Otherwise that "up" feeling for exams would not exist, and most of us depend on that sensation to perform better than usual. However, this anxiety has to be at a level that is manageable.

Of course, as we have just discussed, being prepared for the exam is half the battle right away. Attending all classes, finding out what knowledge will be expected on the exam, and knowing the exam schedules are easy steps to lowering anxiety. Keeping up with work will remove the need to cram, and efficient study habits will eliminate wasted time. Studying should be done in an ideal location for concentration, so that it is simple to become interested in the material and give it complete attention. A method such as SQ3R (Survey, Question, Read, Recite, Review) is a wonderful key to follow to make sure that the study habits are as effective as possible, especially in the case of learning from a textbook. Flashcards are great techniques for memorization. Learning to take good notes will mean that notes will be full of useful information, so that less sifting will need to be done to seek out what is pertinent for studying. Reviewing notes after class and then again on occasion will keep the information fresh in the mind. From notes that have been taken summary sheets and outlines can be made for simpler reviewing.

A study group can also be a very motivational and helpful place to study, as there will be a sharing of ideas, all of the minds can work together, to make sure that everyone understands, and the studying will be made more interesting because it will be a social occasion.

Basically, though, as long as the test-taker remains organized and self confident, with efficient study habits, less time will need to be spent studying, and higher grades will be achieved.

To become self confident, there are many useful steps. The first of these is "self talk." It has been shown through extensive research, that self-talk for students who suffer from test anxiety, should be well monitored, in order to make sure that it contributes to self confidence as opposed to sinking the student. Frequently the self talk of test-anxious students is negative or self-defeating, thinking that everyone else is smarter and faster, that they always mess up, and that if they don't do well, they'll fail the entire course. It is important to decreasing anxiety that awareness is made of self talk. Try writing any negative self thoughts and then disputing them with a positive statement instead. Begin self-encouragement as though it was a friend speaking. Repeat positive statements to help reprogram the mind to believing in successes instead of failures.

Helpful Techniques

Other extremely helpful techniques include:
- Self-visualization of doing well and reaching goals
- While aiming for an "A" level of understanding, don't try to "overprotect" by setting your expectations lower. This will only convince the mind to stop studying in order to meet the lower expectations.
- Don't make comparisons with the results or habits of other students. These are individual factors, and different things work for different people, causing different results.
- Strive to become an expert in learning what works well, and what can be done in order to improve. Consider collecting this data in a journal.
- Create rewards for after studying instead of doing things before studying that will only turn into avoidance behaviors.
- Make a practice of relaxing - by using methods such as progressive relaxation, self-hypnosis, guided imagery, etc - in order to make relaxation an automatic sensation.
- Work on creating a state of relaxed concentration so that concentrating will take on the focus of the mind, so that none will be wasted on worrying.
- Take good care of the physical self by eating well and getting enough sleep.
- Plan in time for exercise and stick to this plan.

Beyond these techniques, there are other methods to be used before, during and after the test that will help the test-taker perform well in addition to overcoming anxiety.

Before the exam comes the academic preparation. This involves establishing a study schedule and beginning at least one week before the actual date of the test. By doing this, the anxiety of not having enough time to study for the test will be automatically eliminated. Moreover, this will make the studying a much more effective experience, ensuring that the learning will be an easier process. This relieves much undue pressure on the test-taker.

Summary sheets, note cards, and flash cards with the main concepts and examples of these main concepts should be prepared in advance of the actual studying time. A topic should never be eliminated from this process. By omitting a topic because it isn't expected to be on the test is only setting up the test-taker for anxiety should it actually appear on the exam. Utilize the course syllabus for laying out the topics that should be studied. Carefully go over the notes that were made in class, paying special attention to any of the issues that the professor took special care to emphasize while lecturing in class. In the textbooks, use the chapter review, or if possible, the chapter tests, to begin your review.

It may even be possible to ask the instructor what information will be covered on the exam, or what the format of the exam will be (for example, multiple choice, essay, free form, true-false). Additionally, see if it is possible to find out how many questions will be on the test. If a review sheet or sample test has been offered by the professor, make good use of it, above anything else, for the preparation for the test. Another great resource for getting to know the examination is reviewing tests from previous semesters. Use these tests to review, and aim to achieve a 100% score on each of the possible topics. With a few exceptions, the goal that you set for yourself is the highest one that you will reach.

Take all of the questions that were assigned as homework, and rework them to any other possible course material. The more problems reworked, the more skill and confidence will form as a result. When forming the solution to a problem, write out each of the steps. Don't simply do head work. By doing as many steps on paper as possible, much clarification and therefore confidence will be formed. Do this with as many homework problems as possible, before checking the answers. By checking the answer after each problem, a reinforcement will exist, that will not be on the exam. Study situations should be as exam-like as possible, to prime the test-taker's system for the experience. By waiting to check the answers at the end, a psychological advantage will be formed, to decrease the stress factor.

Another fantastic reason for not cramming is the avoidance of confusion in concepts, especially when it comes to mathematics. 8-10 hours of study will become one hundred percent more effective if it is spread out over a week or at least several days, instead of doing it all in one sitting. Recognize that the human brain requires time in order to assimilate new material, so frequent breaks and a span of study time over several days will be much more beneficial.

Additionally, don't study right up until the point of the exam. Studying should stop a minimum of one hour before the exam begins. This allows the brain to rest and put things in their proper order. This will also provide the time to become as relaxed as possible when going into the examination room. The test-taker will also have time to eat well and eat sensibly. Know that the brain needs food as much as the rest of the body. With enough food and enough sleep, as well as a relaxed attitude, the body and the mind are primed for success.

Avoid any anxious classmates who are talking about the exam. These students only spread anxiety, and are not worth sharing the anxious sentimentalities.

Before the test also involves creating a positive attitude, so mental preparation should also be a point of concentration. There are many keys to creating a positive attitude. Should fears become rushing in, make a visualization of taking the exam, doing well, and seeing an A written on the paper. Write out a list of affirmations that will bring a feeling of confidence, such as "I am doing well in my English class," "I studied well and know my material," "I enjoy this class." Even if the affirmations aren't believed at first, it sends a positive message to the subconscious which will result in an alteration of the overall belief system, which is the system that creates reality.

If a sensation of panic begins, work with the fear and imagine the very worst! Work through the entire scenario of not passing the test, failing the entire course, and dropping out of school, followed by not getting a job, and pushing a shopping cart through the dark alley where you'll live. This will place things into perspective! Then, practice deep breathing and create a visualization of the opposite situation - achieving an "A" on the exam, passing the entire course, receiving the degree at a graduation ceremony.

On the day of the test, there are many things to be done to ensure the best results, as well as the most calm outlook. The following stages are suggested in order to maximize test-taking potential:

- Begin the examination day with a moderate breakfast, and avoid any coffee or beverages with caffeine if the test taker is prone to jitters. Even people who are used to managing caffeine can feel jittery or light-headed when it is taken on a test day.
- Attempt to do something that is relaxing before the examination begins. As last minute cramming clouds the mastering of overall concepts, it is better to use this time to create a calming outlook.
- Be certain to arrive at the test location well in advance, in order to provide time to select a location that is away from doors, windows and other distractions, as well as giving enough time to relax before the test begins.
- Keep away from anxiety generating classmates who will upset the sensation of stability and relaxation that is being attempted before the exam.
- Should the waiting period before the exam begins cause anxiety, create a self-distraction by reading a light magazine or something else that is relaxing and simple.

During the exam itself, read the entire exam from beginning to end, and find out how much time should be allotted to each individual problem. Once writing the exam, should more time be taken for a problem, it should be abandoned, in order to begin another problem. If there is time at the end, the unfinished problem can always be returned to and completed.

Read the instructions very carefully - twice - so that unpleasant surprises won't follow during or after the exam has ended.

When writing the exam, pretend that the situation is actually simply the completion of homework within a library, or at home. This will assist in forming a relaxed atmosphere, and will allow the brain extra focus for the complex thinking function.

Begin the exam with all of the questions with which the most confidence is felt. This will build the confidence level regarding the entire exam and will begin a quality momentum. This will also create encouragement for trying the problems where uncertainty resides.

Going with the "gut instinct" is always the way to go when solving a problem. Second guessing should be avoided at all costs. Have confidence in the ability to do well.

For essay questions, create an outline in advance that will keep the mind organized and make certain that all of the points are remembered. For multiple choice, read every answer, even if the correct one has been spotted - a better one may exist.

Continue at a pace that is reasonable and not rushed, in order to be able to work carefully. Provide enough time to go over the answers at the end, to check for small errors that can be corrected.

Should a feeling of panic begin, breathe deeply, and think of the feeling of the body releasing sand through its pores. Visualize a calm, peaceful place, and include all of the sights, sounds and sensations of this image. Continue the deep breathing, and take a few minutes to continue this with closed eyes. When all is well again, return to the test.

If a "blanking" occurs for a certain question, skip it and move on to the next question. There will be time to return to the other question later. Get everything done that can be done, first, to guarantee all the grades that can be compiled, and to build all of the confidence possible. Then return to the weaker questions to build the marks from there.

Remember, one's own reality can be created, so as long as the belief is there, success will follow. And remember: anxiety can happen later, right now, there's an exam to be written!

After the examination is complete, whether there is a feeling for a good grade or a bad grade, don't dwell on the exam, and be certain to follow through on the reward that was promised...and enjoy it! Don't dwell on any mistakes that have been made, as there is nothing that can be done at this point anyway.

Additionally, don't begin to study for the next test right away. Do something relaxing for a while, and let the mind relax and prepare itself to begin absorbing information again.

From the results of the exam - both the grade and the entire experience, be certain to learn from what has gone on. Perfect studying habits and work some more on confidence in order to make the next examination experience even better than the last one.

Learn to avoid places where openings occurred for laziness, procrastination and day dreaming.

Use the time between this exam and the next one to better learn to relax, even learning to relax on cue, so that any anxiety can be controlled during the next exam. Learn how to relax the body. Slouch in your chair if that helps. Tighten and then relax all of the different muscle groups, one group at a time, beginning with the feet and then working all the way up to the neck and face. This will ultimately relax the muscles more than they were to begin with. Learn how to breathe deeply and comfortably, and focus on this breathing going in and out as a relaxing thought. With every exhale, repeat the word "relax."

As common as test anxiety is, it is very possible to overcome it. Make yourself one of the test-takers who overcome this frustrating hindrance.

Additional Bonus Material

Due to our efforts to try to keep this book to a manageable length, we've created a link that will give you access to all of your additional bonus material.

Please visit http://www.mometrix.com/bonus948/nystcemath to access the information.